WILLIAM COWPER

WILLIAM COWPER

The Centenary Letters

Edited with an introduction by
SIMON MALPAS

*Fyfield*Books

Published in Great Britain in 2000 by
Carcanet Press Limited
4th Floor, Conavon Court
12–16 Blackfriars Street
Manchester M3 5BQ

A CIP catalogue record for this book
is available from the British Library.

ISBN 1 85754 463 3

The publisher acknowledges financial assistance
from the Arts Council of England.

Set in 10/12pt Palatino by XL Publishing Services, Tiverton
Printed and bound in England by SRP Ltd, Exeter

Contents

Introduction

From the 1840s until the end of the 1970s, interest in William Cowper's poetry was limited almost entirely to specialist scholars, those who shared his evangelical beliefs, and the practising Christians who sang his hymns in church, usually with little or no awareness of his name. With a few notable exceptions, he rarely appeared as more than the representative of a particular group of Christians or the subject of a footnote about eighteenth-century poetry. Today, however, there seems little need to justify republishing Cowper's work for a wider audience. Despite falling into obscurity during the nineteenth century, his writings have recently come to occupy a key position in the English literary canon. Almost all of the anthologies of eighteenth-century and Romantic literature published in the last fifteen years have included significant selections from Cowper's poetry. Scholarly editions of his essays, letters and translations have also recently become available, and two affordable selections of his poems are currently on sale. There is also a growing critical interest in his work and life, with book-length studies by Vincent Newey and Martin Priestman, important discussions by writers such as Marshall Brown and Tim Fulford that link his work to key currents in the development of Romanticism, and a series of interesting biographies. What is, perhaps, surprising today is that his writing ever fell from favour at all. The purpose of this book is to make an affordable selection of Cowper's correspondence available to the growing audience for his work, thereby bringing to a wider readership some of the finest letters written in the English language.

At the beginning of the nineteenth century, Cowper was one of the most popular and widely read poets of his generation. His influence on the early Romantics was extremely powerful. The easy, conversational style that Wordsworth and Coleridge adopted for *Lyrical Ballads* found its model in Cowper's *The Task*, which also lent a series of narrative devices to Wordsworth's *The Prelude*, set the tone of Margaret's emotional desolation in 'The Ruined Cottage', and provided a key source for Coleridge's 'Frost at Midnight'. In *Biographia Literaria*, Coleridge acknowledges his debt, calling Cowper and William Bowles (this latter poet being both influenced by and an advocate of Cowper's writing) the first poets 'who combined natural thought with natural diction; the first who reconciled the heart with the head'.[1] Cowper thus anticipates many of the themes and styles of the early Romantics and, according to Newey, 'without Cowper's example Wordsworth and Coleridge could never have aimed so confidently – with such assurance that what they were doing was both worthwhile and achievable – at, in Coleridge's words, "awakening...attention from the lethargy of custom, and directing it to the loveliness and the wonders of the world before us"'.[2] Without Cowper's example, then, Romanticism might have taken a different course, or at least have had to struggle harder to establish its artistic credentials.

Although his influence on the Romantics now seems indisputable, Cowper's writing is not entirely reducible to this aesthetic movement. Donald Davie argued persuasively in the 1950s that Cowper is much better read as a neo-classical poet working in the shadow of Pope than as an inferior version of Wordsworth. Davie clearly has a point: there is a strong didactic focus that runs through Cowper's writing (the letters as much as the poems), a concern with and talent for classical form, not to mention the almost obligatory Augustan attempt at a translation of Greek or Latin verse (in Cowper's case, Homer's *Iliad* and *Odyssey*, and Milton's Latin poetry). More recently, Brown has asserted that, rather than presenting itself as prophetic of a new artistic movement, Cowper's writing is 'that of a problem-ridden, moody latecomer'.[3]

Reading Cowper as a neo-classical poet is not just a recent invention of academic literary criticism, however. The contrast between Cowper and the full-blooded Romanticism of Wordsworth and Coleridge was noted as early as 1818 by William Hazlitt in his *Lectures on the English Poets*. Hazlitt argues that Cowper, 'seldom launches out into general descriptions of nature: he looks at her over his clipped hedges, and from his well-swept garden-walks... He shakes hands with nature with a pair of fashionable gloves on', and goes on to say that he 'has some of the sickly sensibility and pampered refinements of Pope; but then Pope prided himself in them: whereas Cowper affects to be all simplicity and plainness'.[4] Despite the apparent scorn of Hazlitt's description, there is some accuracy in his analysis: Cowper's poetry frequently refers to and models itself on Pope, and the clipped hedges of *The Task* often have more in common with the ornamental gardens of the eighteenth-century lyric than the wild sublimity of *The Prelude*'s mountains, lakes and gorges. However, as Hazlitt's accusation of 'affectation' might suggest to a more sympathetic reader, Cowper's writing is much more than simply a later version of Pope.

In Cowper's work the neo-classical aesthetic is continually under threat of rupture as the self-revelatory, insecure writing of the Romantic breaks through. At the heart of his poetry lies the individual, tortured consciousness at odds with a hostile world that would soon become a central Romantic figure. The relation between poetry and his mental and emotional insta-bility is stated in a letter to his cousin, Harriot Hesketh: 'dejection of spirits, which I suppose, may have prevented many a man from becoming an author, made me one. I find constant employment necessary, and therefore take care to be constantly employed' (see letter LXV in this collection). The apparent confidence and urbanity of Augustan poetry is disrupted from within by a poetic voice that is often anything but secure or certain. Poetically and historically, then, Cowper stands at the threshold between the neo-classical and the Romantic; he is a vital staging-post in the journey from Pope to Wordsworth and yet is impossible to dismiss as a pale imitator of either.

Not only is this transitional position clear in his poetry, it also appears in his letters. Certainly his distinctive voice is as clearly audible in his correspondence as his poetry, and often the expe-riences of madness and of being forsaken by the God in whom he so fervently believes emerge distinctly in many of his letters. It is for this reason that one of the main causes behind Cowper's disruption of neo-classical writing is frequently sought in his life, which was plagued by bouts of serious depression and mental illness.

Cowper's Life

A passage from Book 3 of *The Task* gives so startlingly clear an account of Cowper's image of himself that David Cecil takes its central image as the title of his biography:

> I was a stricken deer, that left the herd
> Long since: with many an arrow deep infix'd
> My panting side was charged, when I withdrew,
> To seek a tranquil death in distant shades.
> There was I found by one who had himself
> Been hurt by archers. In his side he bore,
> And in his hands and feet cruel scars.
> With gentle force soliciting the darts,
> He drew them forth, and heal'd, and bade me live.
>
> (*The Task*, book 3, 108–16)

Besides the poetry, Cowper's letters and the posthumously published autobiography, *Memoir of the Early Life of William Cowper, Esq.*, which describes his time in London and St Albans, remain the best source of information about his life. However, a brief biography might be useful to set the letters collected here in context.

Cowper was born on 15 December 1731, the fourth (but first surviving) child of the Reverend Dr John and Anne Cowper (*née* Donne). This was a distinguished family: John was the rector of Berkhamstead, and Anne traced her lineage back to Henry III and, it was claimed, John Donne. Other relatives included a leading judge, a general, a number of parliamentary officials, and even (in the figure of William, the first Earl, Cowper) a Lord Chancellor. It was some of these family connections that were eventually to determine Cowper's disastrous decision to embark upon a career in law.

The first great upheaval in the poet's life, however, was the death of his mother in 1737. Cowper recalls this moment in a poem of 1790, 'On the Receipt of My Mother's Picture Out of

Norfolk', inspired by the surprise gift of a miniature portrait of her from his aunt (see letter XCII):

> My mother! when I learn't that thou wast dead,
> Say, wast thou conscious of the tears I shed?
> Hover'd thy spirit o'er thy sorrowing son,
> Wretch even then, life's journey just begun?
> Perhaps thou gav'st me, though unseen, a kiss;
> Perhaps a tear, if souls can weep in bliss –
> Ah that maternal smile! it answers – Yes.
>
> (lines 21–7)

Cowper, aged only six, was crushed by her death and, as biographers such as James King argue, it was the inability to come to terms with his loss that led to bouts of severe depression in later life, as well as the sense of isolation and wretchedness that becomes so apparent in his writing during each of his numerous breakdowns.

Besides his mother, Cowper had problematic relationships with a number of women, although he was to remain unmarried until his death in 1800. While studying as a lawyer in London, he became infatuated with his cousin, Theadora. First, the marriage was forbidden by her father, Ashley Cowper, but when the possibility of Ashley's consent was secured in 1763, Cowper himself refused the match leaving Theadora desolate and subsequently subject to her own descent into mental illness. Another woman with whom Cowper had a sometimes difficult relationship was Lady Ann Austen. Lady Austen often served as the poet's muse, suggesting the poem about a sofa that eventually became *The Task* and providing the anecdote that led Cowper to write the comic poem 'John Gilpin'. They first met in 1781, but by 1782 Cowper had rejected her advances and caused 'mortal offence' (for the poet's account of this, see letter XXXVIII). Although they were eventually reconciled, the relationship between Lady Austen and Cowper was never as intense again.

Perhaps the most important woman in Cowper's life was Mary Unwin, the wife of the Reverend Morley Unwin and mother of William, one of Cowper's chief correspondents.

Cowper looked on Mary as a replacement for his mother, and after they moved to Olney spent his whole life with her, sometimes at risk of scandalising local people who suspected that their relationship was more than platonic. It was Mary who nursed the poet through many of his depressions, and is said to have cut the rope when she found him attempting to hang himself during a period of mental illness in 1787.

Cowper's first, and arguably most crucial, breakdown occurred in 1763 when the offer of a position as Clerk of the Journals for the House of Lords made by his uncle, Ashley Cowper, was challenged and the young man faced the prospect of having his eligibility for the post examined publicly in the House. The impending examination weighed heavily on his mind, and he quickly fell into despondency, beginning to contemplate committing suicide. Things reached such a crisis that, in the days before his trial, Cowper made a number of attempts to kill himself, by drinking laudanum, stabbing himself and, as he described in a passage from his *Memoir*, by hanging:

> I heard the clock strike seven, and instantly it occurred to me that there was no time to be lost. The chambers would soon be opened, and my friend would call upon me to take me with him to Westminster. 'Now is the time', thought I, 'this is the crisis; no more dallying with the love of life'... Not one hesitating thought now remained; but I fell greedily to the execution of my purpose. My garter was made of a broad scarlet binding, with a sliding buckle being sewn together at the end: by the help of the buckle I made a noose... I pushed away the chair with my feet, and hung at my whole length. While I hung there, I distinctly heard a voice say three times, '*'Tis over*!'
>
> (*Memoir of the Early Life of William Cowper Esq.*, 2nd edn 1816, pp. 53–5)

Of course, even this attempt failed: the garter broke and Cowper was rescued by his relations. It was at this point that his career in law ended, although he later retained some links with his legal past when publishing his poetry by writing under the name 'William Cowper of The Inner Temple, Esq.'. Seeing his growing despondency, and fearing further attempts on his own life, his relatives eventually committed Cowper to Doctor Cotton's 'Collegium Insanorum' in St Albans.

It was during his stay at Cotton's that Cowper, who in the depths of his depression had thought himself cast out from God, became a convinced evangelical Christian. Again, his description of this in the *Memoir* is well worth noting:

> I flung myself into a chair near the window, and seeing a Bible there, ventured once more to apply to it for comfort and instruction. The first verse I saw, was the 25th of the 3rd of Romans... Immediately I received the strength to believe, and the full beams of the Sun of Righteousness shone upon me. I saw the sufficiency of the atonement he [Christ] had made, my pardon sealed in his blood, and all the fullness and completeness of his justification. In a moment I believed and received the gospel.

> *(Memoir, pp. 77–8)*

After this moment of revelation, Cowper's religious conversion progressed gradually as he was nurtured back to health by Cotton, and then the Unwin family when he moved to Huntingdon. His faith was strengthened even further by a new acquaintance he made on his arrival at Olney in September 1767, the Evangelical preacher John Newton.

Newton himself had gone through a similar process of revelation. He started out as a slave trader, but after surviving a ferocious storm at sea converted and became an energetic and fervent evangelist. With Newton, Cowper wrote the *Olney Hymns* which was published in 1779. The hymns were immensely popular and appeared in almost thirty new editions over the next fifty years. Among the most memorable of Cowper's contributions to this volume are 'The Contrite Heart', 'Contentment' and 'Light Shining out of Darkness', all of which continue to be sung regularly today. Newton remained a life-long correspondent, and also gave advice to the poet on the subjects of many of his later works.

From the time he moved to Olney with the widowed Mrs

Unwin (her husband having died suddenly in a riding accident), Cowper lived a life of retreat from the cosmopolitan bustle of the eighteenth-century world. His main contacts with the outside were his poetry and, of course, the letters he sent to and received from friends and members of his family. This life is only discussed briefly in the final paragraph of the *Memoir*, which ends with his arrival in Olney:

> I took possession of my new abode, Nov. 11, 1765. I have found it a place of rest prepared for me by God's own hand, where he has blessed me with a thousand mercies, and instances of his fatherly protection; and where he has given me furtherance in the knowledge of our Lord Jesus, both by the study of his own word, and communion with his dear disciples. May nothing but death interrupt our union!
>
> (*Memoir*, pp. 91–2)

In fact, Olney and the nearby Weston Underwood, to which Cowper and Mrs Unwin moved in 1786, did remain his 'place of rest' until he was taken into care during his final illness and depression which began in 1795.

Although the tone of Cowper's *Memoir* sometimes has an awkward piety stemming from his recent conversion, the insights it offers into his thoughts and feelings are invaluable. Once the *Memoir* ends, however, the best source of biography for Cowper's later life are the letters. He describes everyday events, moods and impressions; he speculates about current events and charts the political upheavals of his time; and, perhaps most importantly for a modern reader, offers many intriguing insights into the composition and reception of his poetry.

Cowper published his first volume, entitled simply *Poems*, in 1782. This volume is made up of eight moral satires and a larger number of shorter pieces. Although the reviews were mixed, Cowper was highly satisfied with them. Of particular interest is the glowing review in a letter he received from Benjamin Franklin (see letter XL). Encouraged by the reception of his work, Cowper began a second volume which would eventually come to be made up almost entirely of *The Task*. Consisting of six long books, *The Task* is Cowper's most successful and complex poem. It is a loosely constructed progress that skips quickly and easily from conversational to epic, parodic and devotional verse. Beginning with a mock-epic description of the evolution of the sofa, it explores subjects as diverse as nature, domestic life, slavery, growing cucumbers, madness and divinity.

Having completed *The Task*, Cowper turned his attention to the classics, embarking on a translation of Homer's *Iliad* and *Odyssey*. In undertaking this project, Cowper was directly pitting himself against Pope's earlier translations. The descriptions in his letters of the differences between his translation and Pope's show as clearly as any other comments Cowper's problematic relation with neo-classical poetry. His statement of intent in a letter to Harriot Hesketh presents an apt example of the way Cowper's discussions of translation begin to generate a complex account of his idea of aesthetics:

> Except the Bible, there never was in the world a book so remarkable for that species of the sublime that owes its very existence to simplicity, as the works of Homer. He is always nervous, plain, natural... The garden in all the gaiety of June is less flowery than his [Pope's} Translation. Metaphors of which Homer never dreamt, which he did not seek, and which probably he would have disdained if he had found, follow each other in quick succession like the sliding pictures in a show box.
>
> (to Lady Hesketh, 15 December 1785; letter LXVIII)

The translations took a great deal longer than Cowper at first suspected they would but, again, they kept his depression at bay, and also allowed him to re-establish contact with many of his old friends as they joined the subscription list for his volume.

Cowper's final, unfinished, project was to prepare an edition of Milton's poetry that would be illustrated by the painter, Henry Fuseli. However, the deepening depression of the 1790s put paid to this, and he made very little progress before his death in 1800.

Cowper's Letters

Cowper's letters are a constant and often surprising source of information about his life and work. However, they are interesting not simply because of their biographical detail or the insights they offer into the process of poetic composition, they have great literary merit of their own. Cowper could write just as fascinatingly about the completely mundane as he could about events of great moment and import: '[A] letter may be written on anything or nothing just as that anything or nothing happens to occur' (to William Unwin on 6 August 1780; letter XXII). That Cowper's letters remain fascinating documents two hundred years after his death might at first seem surprising. His life, when judged by any objective standards, was largely uneventful: he did not travel widely, was not present at the great events of his time, and never became deeply embroiled in the myriad political intrigues and revolutions of the age. In fact, after his first breakdown, most of his life was spent in retirement from the metropolitan centres of the eighteenth-century world. Reading his letters at the beginning of the twenty-first century, though, it is difficult to escape the conclusion that he still appears a resolutely modern figure. Through their focus on the everyday domestic concerns of somebody living in a small community, often at a distance from his friends and family, the letters generate a sense of an individual at sea in a world that is beyond his control, but one who accepts that position with alternating bouts of humour and anxiety. For us, perhaps, it is the means that Cowper finds to deal with, or often not deal with, this sense of alienation which makes his writing appear so prescient of the concerns of our contemporary life. This ability to draw out the varied nuances of the everyday situation and to speculate both wittily and intelligently about the world at large is a key reason why Cowper remains to this day one of the greatest epistolary writers in the English language.

The range of issues and ideas discussed in his letters is too vast to summarise here. From the political upheaval of the Gordon Riots and French revolution, through the invention of the hot-air balloon and the fight against slavery, to the minutiae of domestic life, Cowper casts a telling eye over the closing years of the eighteenth century. And not only is the range of subjects vast, the myriad styles in which they are covered is often breathtaking. Cowper's writing is as eloquent in giving spiritual advice to younger friends as it is in telling jokes about philosophers becoming balloons by inflating themselves with the hot air of their own ideas. The tone of hope about the release of a new volume of poems is as striking as the agony of the final letters as he sinks into his last bout of illness.

However, the letters are not formal or planned in the style often associated with the *belles lettres*. Rather, as Cowper himself takes pains to explain, they follow the spontaneous flow of a conversation:

> A letter is written as a conversation is maintained, or a journey is performed; not by preconcerted or premeditated means, a new contrivance, or an invention never heard of before, – but merely by maintaining a progress, and resolving as a postilion does, having once set out, never to stop till we reach the appointed end.
>
> (To William Unwin on 6 August 1780; letter XXII)

This unpremeditated conversational progress, so like the narrative style of his most original poem, *The Task*, makes Cowper's observation and argument so continually fresh and surprising that his insights into even the most trivial domestic matters remain hauntingly striking two hundred years after his death.

King's and Ryskamp's standard scholarly edition of the letters runs to five long volumes, and the process of selecting from Cowper's correspondence that I have undertaken here has been guided by two principles. I have attempted, first, to present letters from each of the different periods of his adult life, and to demonstrate the variety and vitality of his modes of addressing his different correspondents. These range from the pious and sometimes slightly moralistic early letters to Maria Cowper and John Newton, to the vibrancy and inventiveness of his correspondence with Joseph Hill and William Unwin, and the despondency of the final letters to Harriot Hesketh. My second principle has been, as often as possible, to use complete letters. Despite his arguments about writing without a premed-

xvii

itated purpose, Cowper's letters are frequently as beautifully constructed as his poems, and can only benefit from being read in their entirety.

Notes

1 Samuel Taylor Coleridge, *Biographia Literaria*, eds James Engel and W. Jackson Bate (Princeton, N.J.: Princeton University Press, 1983), p. 25.
2 Vincent Newey, *Cowper's Poetry: A Critical Study and Reassessment* (Liverpool: Liverpool University Press, 1982), p. 9.
3 Marshall Brown, *Preromanticism* (Stanford, Calif.: Stanford University Press, 1991), p. 59.
4 William Hazlitt, 'On Thomson and Cowper', in *Lectures on the English Poets* (1818), from P.P. Howe, ed., *The Complete Works of William Hazlitt*, vol. 5, (London: J.M. Dent, 1930–4), p. 92.

Acknowledgements

This selection is based on two texts. Most of the letters are taken from J.S. Memes's *The Letters of William Cowper*, 1845; while the remainder are from J.G. Frazer's *The Letters of William Cowper*, 1912.

I should like to thank Michael Schmidt for his assistance with the preparation of this edition, and the frequently enlightening ideas about Cowper's work that he has offered. I have also received advice, support and encouragement from Erikka Askeland, Barry Atkins, Angelica Michaelis and Jo Smith, to all of whom I am extremely grateful.

Further Reading

Two of the most readily available selections of William Cowper's poetry are:

Michael Bruce, ed., *William Cowper*, London: J.M. Dent, 1999.
James Sambrook, ed., *The Task and Selected Other Poems*, London: Longman, 1994.

The standard scholarly edition of the poems is:
John D. Baird and Charles Ryskamp, eds, *The Poems of William Cowper*, 3 vols, Oxford: Clarendon Press, 1980–95.

For a complete collection of Cowper's letters, see:
James King and Charles Ryskamp, eds, *The Letters and Prose Writings of William Cowper*, 5 vols, Oxford: Clarendon Press, 1979–86.

Some useful and interesting biographies are:
David Cecil, *The Stricken Deer*, London: Constable, 1988.
James King, *William Cowper: A Biography*, Durham, N.C.: Duke University Press, 1986.
Charles Ryskamp, *William Cowper of the Inner Temple, Esq.*, Cambridge: Cambridge University Press, 1959.

Criticism:
Marshall Brown, *Preromanticism*, Stanford, Calif.: Stanford University Press, 1991.
Leonore Davidoff and Catherine Hall, *Family Fortunes*, London: Hutchinson, 1987.
Richard Feingold, *Nature and Society*, New Brunswick, N.J.: Rutgers University Press, 1978.
William Free, *William Cowper*, New York: Twayne Publishers, 1970.
Tim Fulford, *Landscape, Liberty and Authority*, Cambridge: Cambridge University Press, 1996.
Vincent Newey, *Cowper's Poetry: A Critical Study and*

Reassessment, Liverpool: Liverpool University Press, 1982.

Martin Priestman, *Cowper's Task: Structure and Influence*, Cambridge: Cambridge University Press, 1983.

Patricia Meyer Spacks, *The Poetry of Vision*, Cambridge, Mass.: Harvard University Press, 1967.

In August 1763, William Cowper was busily studying to become Clerk of the Journals in the House of Lords. Ashley Cowper, the poet's uncle, had offered this position, but his right of appointment had been challenged by a rival faction. The stressful anticipation of an impending examination at the bar of the House would lead Cowper to a nervous breakdown.

The addressee of this letter, Lady Harriot Hesketh, is Cowper's cousin, and the eldest daughter of Ashley Cowper. Later, Lady Hesketh would become one of his chief patrons and correspondents. Cowper's statement that he wonders why he was never in love with her is somewhat ironic as he had been in love with, and come close to marrying, her sister Theodora, in 1756. At about the time of this letter, Cowper was in the process of rejecting a second marriage proposal, which left Theodora devastated.

My Dear Cousin,

Having promised to write to you, I make haste to be as good as my word. I have a pleasure in writing to you at any time, but especially at the present, when my days are spent in reading the Journals, and my nights in dreaming of them. An employment not very agreeable to a head that has long been habituated to the luxury of choosing its subject, and has been as little employed upon business, as if it had grown upon the shoulders of a much wealthier gentleman. But the numskull pays for it now, and will not presently forget the discipline it has undergone lately. If I succeed in this doubtful piece of promotion, I shall have at least this satisfaction to reflect upon, that the volumes I write will be treasured up with the utmost care for ages, and will last as long as the English constitution, – a duration which ought to satisfy the vanity of any author who has a spark of love for his country. O! my good cousin! if I was to open my heart to you, I could show you strange sights; nothing, I flatter myself, that would shock you, but a great deal that would make you wonder. I am of a very singular temper, and very unlike all the men that I have ever conversed with. Certainly I am not an absolute fool; but I have more weakness than the greatest of all the fools I can recollect at present. In short, if I was as fit for the next world, as I am unfit for this, – and God forbid I should speak it in vanity! I would not change conditions with any saint in Christendom.

My destination is settled at last, and I have obtained a furlough. Margate is the word, and what do you think will ensue, cousin? I know what you expect, but ever since I was born I have been good at disappointing the most natural expectations. Many years ago, cousin, there was a possibility I might prove a very different thing from what I am at present. My character is now fixed, and riveted fast upon me; and, between friends, it is not a very splendid one, or likely to be guilty of much fascination.

Adieu, my dear cousin! So much as I love you, I wonder how the deuce it has happened I was never in love with you. Thank Heaven that I never was, for at this time I have had a pleasure in writing to you, which in that case I should have forfeited. Let me hear from you, or I shall reap but half the reward that is due to my noble indifference. – Yours ever, and evermore,

W.C.

II *To Joseph Hill* 24 June 1765

Following the breakdown of 1763, Cowper was taken to an asylum run by Dr Nathaniel Cotton in St Albans, where he remained until 17 June 1765. On his release, Cowper moved to Huntingdon, taking a servant, Samuel Roberts, who would remain with him for the next thirty years. Joseph Hill, a lawyer, was one of Cowper's closest friends during his time in London and for the rest of the poet's life, as well as a significant benefactor during his periods of poverty.

The 'Turkish spy' alludes to *Letters Writ by a Turkish Spy* by Giovanni Marana which contains the statement, 'And because I will have no enemy near me, I will therefore admit of no servant'. Fluellen is the Welsh captain in Shakespeare's *Henry V*; Cowper cites Act 4, scene 7, lines 31–2.

Dear Joe,

The only recompense I can make you for your kind attention to my affairs during my illness, is to tell you, that by the mercy of God I am restored to perfect health both of mind and body. This I believe will give you pleasure; and I would gladly do any thing from which you could receive it.

I left St Alban's on the seventeenth, and arrived that day at Cambridge, spent some time there with my brother, and came hither on the twenty-second. I have a lodging that puts me continually in mind of our summer excursions; we have had many worse, and except the size of it, (which however is sufficient for a single man,) but few better. I am not quite alone, having brought a servant with me from St Alban's, who is the very mirror of fidelity and affection for his master. And whereas the Turkish Spy says, he kept no servant, because he would not have an enemy in his house, I hired mine, because I would have a friend. Men do not usually bestow these encomiums on their lackeys, nor do they usually deserve them; but I have had experience of mine, both in sickness and in health, and never saw his fellow.

The river Ouse, (I forget how they spell it,) is the most agreeable circumstance in this part of the world; at this town it is I believe as wide as the Thames at Windsor; nor does the silver Thames better deserve that epithet, nor has it more flowers upon its banks, these being attributes which in strict truth belong to neither. Fluellin would say, they are as like as my fingers to my fingers, and there is salmon in both. It is a noble stream to bath in, and I shall make that use of it three times a week, having introduced myself to it for the first time this morning.

I beg you will remember me to all my friends, which is a task will cost you no great pains to execute: particularly remember

3

me to those of your own house, and believe me, your very affectionate,

W.C.

III *To Lady Hesketh* 1 July 1765

My Dear Lady Hesketh,

Since the visit you were so kind as to pay me in the Temple (the only time I ever saw you without pleasure), what have I not suffered! And since it has pleased God to restore me to the use of my reason, what have I not enjoyed! You know, by experience, how pleasant it is to feel the first approaches of health after a fever; but, Oh the fever of the brain! To feel the quenching of that fire is indeed a blessing which I think it impossible to receive without the most consummate gratitude. Terrible as this chastisement is, I acknowledge in it the hand of an infinite justice: nor is it at all more difficult for me to perceive in it the hand of an infinite mercy likewise: when I consider the effect it has had upon me, I am exceedingly thankful for it, and, without hypocrisy, esteem it the greatest blessing, next to life itself, I ever received from the divine bounty. I pray God that I may ever retain this sense of it, and then I am sure I shall continue to be, as I am at present, really happy.

I write thus to you that you may not think me a forlorn and wretched creature; which you might be apt to do, considering my very distant removal from every friend I have in the world; a circumstance which, before this event befell me, would undoubtedly have made me so: but my affliction has taught me a road to happiness which without it I should never have found; and I know, and have experience of it every day, that the mercy of God, to him who believes himself the object of it, is more than sufficient to compensate for the loss of every other blessing.

You may now inform all those whom you think really interested in my welfare, that they have no need to be apprehensive on the score of my happiness at present. And you yourself will believe that my happiness is no dream, because I have told you

4

the foundation on which it is built. What I have written would appear like enthusiasm to many, for we are apt to give that name to every warm affection of the mind in others which we have not experienced in ourselves; but to you, who have so much to be thankful for, and a temper inclined to gratitude, it will not appear so.

I beg you will give my love to Sir Thomas, and believe that I am obliged to you both for inquiring after me, at St Alban's.

Yours ever,

W.C.

IV *To Lady Hesketh*   14 September 1765

This letter introduces some of the people Cowper met during his time in Huntingdon. The most notable of these are the Unwins. The Reverend Morley Unwin, retired headmaster of Huntingdon School, and his wife Mary had two children: William and Susanna. To avoid financial hardship, Cowper was to move in with the Unwins in November 1765 (see letter VI). Mary and William Unwin quickly became two of the mainstays of Cowper's life.

My Dear Cousin,

The longer I live here, the better I like the place, and the people who belong to it. I am upon very good terms with no less than five families, besides two or three odd scrambling fellows like myself. The last acquaintance I made here is with the race of the Unwins, consisting of father and mother, son and daughter, the most comfortable social folks you ever knew. The son is about twenty-one years of age, one of the most unreserved and amiable young men I ever conversed with. He is not yet arrived at that time of life, when suspicion recommends itself to us in the form of wisdom, and sets every thing but our own dear selves at an immeasurable distance from our esteem and confidence. Consequently he is known almost as soon as seen, and having nothing in his heart that makes it necessary for him to keep it barred and bolted, opens it to the perusal even of a stranger. The father is a clergyman, and the son is designed for orders. The design, however, is quite his own, proceeding merely from his being and having always been sincere in his belief and love of the Gospel. Another acquaintance I have lately made is with a Mr Nicholson, a North country divine, very poor, but very good, and very happy. He reads prayers here twice a day, all the year round; and travels on foot to serve two churches every Sunday through the year, his journey out and home again being sixteen miles. I supped with him last night. He gave me bread and cheese, and a black jug of ale of his own brewing, and doubtless brewed by his own hands. Another of my acquaintance is Mr—, a thin, tall, old man, and as good as he is thin. He drinks nothing but water, and eats no flesh; partly (I believe) from a religious scruple (for he is very religious), and partly in the spirit of a valetudinarian. He is to be met with every morning of his life, at about six o'clock, at a FOUNTAIN of very fine water, about a mile from the town, which is reckoned extremely like the Bristol spring. Being both early risers, and the only early walkers in the place, we soon became acquainted. His great piety can be equalled by nothing but his great regularity, for he is the most perfect time-piece in the world. I have received a visit likewise from Mr —. He is very much a gentleman, well read, and sensible. I am persuaded, in short, that if I had the choice of all England, where to fix my abode, I could not have chosen better for myself, and most likely I should not have chosen so well.

[...]

Yours ever,
W.C.

V *To Lady Hesketh*   18 October 1765

I wish you joy, my dear cousin, of being safely arrived in port from the storms of Southampton. For my own part, who am but as a Thames wherry, in a world full of tempest and commotion,

I know so well the value of the creek I have put into, and the snugness it affords me, that I have a sensible sympathy with you in the pleasure you find in being once more blown to Droxford. I know enough of Miss Morley to send her my compliments; to which, if I had never seen her, her affection for you would sufficiently entitle her. If I neglected to do it sooner, it is only because I am naturally apt to neglect what I ought to do; and if I was as genteel as I am negligent, I should be the most delightful creature in the universe.

I am glad you think so favourably of my Huntingdon acquaintance; they are indeed a nice set of folks, and suit me exactly. I should have been more particular in my account of Miss Unwin, if I had had materials for a minute description. She is about eighteen years of age, rather handsome and genteel. In her mother's company she says little; not because her mother requires it of her, but because she seems glad of that excuse for not talking, being somewhat inclined to bashfulness. There is the most remarkable cordiality between all the parts of the family; and the mother and daughter seem to dote upon each other. The first time I went to the house I was introduced to the daughter alone; and sat with her near half an hour, before her brother came in, who had appointed me to call upon him. Talking is necessary in a tête-a-tête, to distinguish the persons of the drama from the chairs they sit on: accordingly she talked a great deal, and extremely well; and, like the rest of the family, behaved with as much ease of address as if we had been old acquaintance. She resembles her mother in her great piety, who is one of the most remarkable instances of it I have ever seen. They are altogether the cheerfulest and most engaging family-piece it is possible to conceive.

Since I wrote the above, I met Mrs Unwin in the street, and went home with her. She and I walked together near two hours in the garden, and had a conversation which did me more good than I should have received from an audience of the first prince in Europe. That woman is a blessing to me, and I never see her without being the better for her company. I am treated in the family as if I was a near relation, and have been repeatedly invited to call upon them at all times. You know what a shy fellow I am; I cannot prevail with myself to make so much use of this privilege as I am sure they intend I should; but perhaps this awkwardness will wear off hereafter. It was my earnest request before I left St Alban's, that wherever it might please Providence to dispose of me, I might meet with such an acquaintance as I find in Mrs Unwin. How happy it is to believe, with a steadfast assurance, that our petitions are heard even while we are making them; and how delightful to meet with a proof of it in the effectual and actual grant of them! Surely it is a gracious finishing given to those means, which the Almighty has been pleased to make use of for my conversion. After having been deservedly rendered unfit for any society, to be again qualified for it, and admitted at once into the fellowship of those whom God regards as the excellent of the earth, and whom, in the emphatical language of Scripture, he preserves as the apple of his eye, is a blessing which carries with it the stamp and visible superscription of divine bounty, – a grace unlimited as undeserved; and like its glorious Author, free in its course, and blessed in its operation!

My dear cousin! health and happiness, and above all, the favour of our great and gracious Lord, attend you! While we seek it in spirit and in truth, we are infinitely more secure of it than of the next breath we expect to draw. Heaven and earth have their destined periods; ten thousand worlds will vanish at the consummation of all things; but the word of God standeth fast; and they who trust in him shall never be confounded. My love to all who inquire after me.

– Yours affectionately,

W.C.

VI *To Joseph Hill*   5 November 1765

Dear Joe,
    I wrote to you about ten days ago,
        Soliciting a quick return of gold,
            to purchase certain horse that like me well.

Either my letter or your answer to it, I fear, has miscarried. The former, I hope; because a miscarriage of the latter might be attended with bad consequences.

I find it impossible to proceed any longer in my present course, without danger of bankruptcy. I have therefore entered into an agreement with the Rev. Mr Unwin, to lodge and board with him. The family are the most agreeable in the world. They live in a special good house, and in a very genteel way. They are exactly what I would wish them to be, and I know I shall be as happy with them as I can be on this side of the sun. I did not dream of this matter till about five days ago: but now the whole is settled. I shall transfer myself thither as soon as I have satisfied all demands upon me here.

– Yours ever,

W.C.

[...]

VII *To Mrs Cowper*   11 March 1766

The addressee of this letter is Maria Cowper (*née* Madan), Cowper's cousin. The Martin who is referred to is her brother who was a close friend of Cowper's during his time in London, and was with him at the time of his breakdown.

My Dear Cousin,

I am much obliged to you for Pearsall's Meditations, especially as it furnishes me with an occasion of writing to you, which is all I have waited for. My friends must excuse me, if I write to none but those who lay it fairly in my way to do so. The inference I am apt to draw from their silence is, that they wish *me* to be silent too.

I have great reason, my dear cousin, to be thankful to the gracious Providence that conducted me to this place. The lady in whose house I live, is so excellent a person, and regards me with a friendship so truly Christian, that I could almost fancy my own mother restored to life again, to compensate to me for all the friends I have lost, and all my connections broken. She has a son at Cambridge, in all respects worthy of such a mother, the most amiable young man I ever knew. His natural and acquired endowments are very considerable; and as to his virtues, I need only say, that he is a Christian. It ought to be a matter of daily thanksgiving to me, that I am admitted into the society of such persons; and I pray God to make me and keep me worthy of them.

Your brother Martin has been very kind to me, having written to me twice in a style which, though it was once irksome to me, to say the least, I now know how to value. I pray God to forgive me the many light things I have both said and thought of him and his labours. Hereafter I shall consider him as a burning and shining light, and as one of those 'who, having turned many to righteousness, shall shine hereafter as the stars for ever and ever.'

So much for the state of my heart; as to my spirits, I am cheerful and happy, and, having peace with God, have peace within myself. For the continuance of this blessing, I trust to Him who gives it; and they who trust in Him shall never be confounded. – Yours affectionately,

W.C.

VIII *To Mrs Cowper*   20 October 1766

My Dear Cousin,

[…]

I am obliged to you for the interest you take in my welfare, and for your inquiring so particularly after the manner in which my time passes here. As to amusements, I mean what the world calls such, we have none; the place indeed swarms with them, and cards and dancing are the professed business of almost all the *gentle* inhabitants of Huntingdon. We refuse to take part in them, or to be accessaries to this way of murdering our time, and by so doing have acquired the name of Methodists. Having told you how we *do not* spend our time, I will next say how we do. We breakfast commonly between eight and nine; till eleven, we read either the Scripture, or the sermons of some faithful preacher of those holy mysteries; at eleven we attend divine service, which is performed here twice every day; and from twelve to three we separate and amuse ourselves as we please. During that interval I either read in my own apartment, or walk, or ride, or work in the garden. We seldom sit an hour after dinner, but if the weather permits adjourn to the garden, where with Mrs Unwin and her son I have generally the pleasure of religious conversation till tea-time. If it rains, or is too windy for walking, we either converse within doors, or sing some hymns of Martin's collection, and by the help of Mrs Unwin's harpsichord make up a tolerable concert, in which our hearts, I hope, are the best and most musical performers. After tea we sally forth to walk in good earnest. Mrs Unwin is a good walker, and we have generally travelled about four miles before we see home again. When the days are short, we make this excursion in the former part of the day, between church-time and dinner. At night we read and converse, as before, till supper, and commonly finish the evening either with hymns or a sermon; and last of all the family are called to prayers. I need not tell *you*, that such a life as this is consistent with the utmost cheerfulness; accordingly we are all happy, and dwell together in unity as brethren. Mrs Unwin has almost a maternal affection for me, and I have something very like a filial one for her, and her son and I are brothers. Blessed be the God of our salvation for such companions, and for such a life; above all, for a heart to like it.

I have had many anxious thoughts about taking orders, and I believe every new convert is apt to think himself called upon for that purpose; but it has pleased God, by means which there is no need to particularize, to give me full satisfaction as to the propriety of declining it; indeed, they who have the least idea of what I have suffered from the dread of public exhibitions, will readily excuse my never attempting them hereafter. In the meantime, if it please the Almighty, I may be an instrument of turning many to the truth in a private way, and I hope that my endeavours in this way have not been entirely unsuccessful.

Had I the zeal of Moses, I should want an Aaron to be my spokesman.–Yours ever, my dear cousin,

W.C.

IX *To Mrs Cowper*   13 July 1767

My Dear Cousin,

The newspaper has told you the truth. Poor Mr Unwin being flung from his horse, as he was going to the church on Sunday morning, received a dreadful fracture on the back part of the skull, under which he languished till Thursday evening, and then died. This awful dispensation has left an impression upon our spirits which will not presently be worn off. He died in a poor cottage, to which he was carried immediately after his fall about a mile from home; and his body could not be brought to his house till the spirit was gone to Him who gave it. May it be a lesson to us to watch, since we know not the day nor the hour when our Lord cometh!

The effect of it upon my circumstances will only be a change of the place of my abode. For I shall still, by God's leave, continue with Mrs Unwin, whose behaviour to me has always been that of a mother to a son. We know not yet where we shall settle, but we trust that the Lord, whom we seek, will go before us, and prepare a rest for us. We have employed our friend Haweis, Dr Conyers of Helmsley in Yorkshire, and Mr Newton of Olney, to look out a place for us, but at present are entirely ignorant under which of the three we shall settle, or whether under either. I have written to my Aunt Madan, to desire Martin to assist us with his enquiries. It is probable we shall stay here till Michaelmas.

W. C.

The Move to Olney
Following Mr Unwin's death, Cowper, Mrs Unwin and her daughter moved to Olney with the assistance of the Reverend John Newton, the evangelical curate of the small town. Arriving

12

in Olney on 14 September 1767, they stayed with the Newtons while a house, Orchardside, was being prepared for them, eventually moving there on 15 February 1768. John Newton and his wife became close friends with Cowper, the former collaborating with him on *Olney Hymns* and frequently offering advice on the composition and publication of his other poetry.

X *To William Unwin*   31 March 1770

On 20 March 1770 Cowper's brother John died after a long illness. Cowper travelled to visit him in Cambridge in February, and remained with him until his death. This letter describes the poet's relief that this brother converted before passing away.

My Dear Friend,
I am glad that the Lord made you a fellow-labourer with us in praying my dear brother out of darkness into light. It was a blessed work; and when it shall be your turn to die in the Lord, and to rest from all your labours, that work shall follow you. I once entertained hopes of his recovery: from the moment when it pleased God to give him light in his soul, there was, for four days, such a visible amendment in his body as surprised us all. Dr Glynn himself was puzzled, and began to think that all his threatening conjectures would fail of their accomplishment. I am well satisfied that it was thus ordered, not for his own sake, but for the sake of us, who had been so deeply concerned for his spiritual welfare, that he might be able to give such evident proof of the work of God upon his soul as should leave no doubt behind it. As to his friends at Cambridge, they knew nothing of the matter. He never spoke of these things but to myself; nor to me, when others were within hearing, except that he sometimes would speak in the presence of the nurse. He knew well to make the distinction between those who could understand him, and those who could not; and that he was not in circumstances to

maintain such a controversy as a declaration of his new views and sentiments would have exposed him to. Just after his death, I spoke of this change to a dear friend of his, a fellow of the college, who had attended him through all his sickness with assiduity and tenderness. But he did not understand me.

I now proceed to mention such particulars as I can recollect, and which I had not opportunity to insert in my letters to Olney; for I left Cambridge suddenly, and sooner than I expected. He was deeply impressed with a sense of the difficulties he should have to encounter, if it should please God to raise him again. He saw the necessity of being faithful, and the opposition he should expose himself to by being so. Under the weight of these thoughts, he one day broke out in the following prayer, when only myself was with him. 'O Lord, thou art light; and in thee is no darkness at all. Thou art the fountain of all wisdom, and it is essential to thee to be good and gracious. I am a child, O Lord, teach me how I shall conduct myself! Give me the wisdom of the serpent with the harmlessness of the dove! Bless the souls thou hast committed to the care of thy helpless miserable creature, who has no wisdom or knowledge of his own, and make me faithful to them for thy mercy's sake!' Another time he said, 'How wonderful it is, that God should look upon man; and how much more wonderful that he should look upon such a worm as I am! Yet he does look upon me, and takes the exactest notice of all my sufferings. He is present, and I see him, (I mean, by faith;) and he stretches out his arms towards me,' – and he then stretched out his own – 'and he says, "Come unto me, all ye that are weary and heavy laden, and I will give you rest!"' He smiled and wept, when he spoke these words. When he expressed himself upon these subjects, there was a weight and a dignity in his manner such as I never saw before. He spoke with the greatest deliberation, making a pause at the end of every sentence; and there was something in his air and in the tone of his voice, inexpressibly solemn, unlike himself, unlike what I had ever seen in another.

This hath God wrought. I have praised him for his marvellous act, and have felt a joy of heart upon the subject of my brother's death, such as I never felt but in my own conversion.

He is now before the throne; and yet a little while and we shall meet, never more to be divided. – Yours, my very dear friend, with my affectionate respects to yourself and yours,

William Cowper

Postscript. – A day or two before his death, he grew so weak and was so very ill, that he required continual attendance, so that he had neither strength nor opportunity to say much to me. Only, the day before, he said he had had a sleepless, but a composed and quiet night. I asked him, if he had been able to collect his thoughts. He replied, 'All night long I have endeavoured to think upon God and to continue in prayer. I have great peace and comfort; and what comfort I had came in that way.' When I saw him the next morning at seven o'clock he was dying, fast asleep, and exempted, in all appearance, from the sense of those pangs which accompany dissolution. I shall be glad to hear from you, my dear friend, when you can find time to write, and are so inclined. The death of my beloved brother teems with many useful lessons. May God seal the instruction upon our hearts!

XI *To W. Unwin*   18 July 1778

My Dear Friend,

I hurry you into the midst of things at once, which if it be not much in the epistolary style, is acknowledged however to be very sublime. Mr Morley, videlicet the grocer, is guilty of much neglect and carelessness, and has lately so much disappointed your mother, that she is at last obliged to leave him, and begs you will send her Mr Rawlinson's address, that she may transfer her custom to him. She adds, moreover, that she was well aware of the unseasonableness of salmon at this time, and did not mean that you should order any to Olney till the spring.

We are indebted to you for your political intelligence, but have it not in our power to pay you in kind. Proceed, however, to give us such information as cannot be learned from the newspaper; and when any thing arises at Olney, that is not in the threadbare style of daily occurrences, you shall hear of it in return. Nothing of this sort has happened lately, except that a lion was imported here at the fair, seventy years of age, and was as tame as a goose. Your mother and I saw him embrace his keeper with his paws, and lick his face. Others saw him receive his head in his mouth, and restore it to him again unhurt; – a sight we chose not to be favoured with, but rather advised the honest man to discontinue the practice, – a practice hardly reconcilable to prudence, unless he had a head to spare. The beast, however, was a very magnificent one, and much more royal in his appearance than those I have seen in the Tower.

[...]

Your mother joins me in affectionate respects – I should have said love, to yourself, Mrs Unwin, Miss Shuttleworth, and little John. If you will accept this for a letter, perhaps I may be able to furnish you with more such upon occasion. – Yours, with thanks for your last,

Wm Cowper

XII *To William Unwin* 26 May 1779

The book referred to in both this and the next letter is Samuel Johnson's *Lives of the English Poets*, the first four volumes of which were published in 1779. Johnson, perhaps the most influential literary figure of his age, was a constant source of interest and worry for Cowper, particularly with regard to what the critic's view of his own work might be.

My Dear Friend,

[...]

I am obliged to you for the Poets; [...] I have looked into some of the volumes, but not having yet finished the *Register* have merely looked into them. A few things I have met with, which if they had been burned the moment they were written, it would have been better for the author, and at least as well for his readers. There is not much of this, but a little is too much. I think it a pity the editor admitted any; the English Muse would have lost no credit by the omission of such trash. Some of them again seem to me to have but a very disputable right to a place among the Classics; and I am quite at a loss, when I see them in such company, to conjecture what is Dr Johnson's idea or definition of classical merit. But if he inserts the poems of some who can hardly be said to deserve such an honour, the purchaser may comfort himself with the hope that he will exclude none that do.

Your mother sends her love and affectionate remembrance to all at Stock, from the tallest to the shortest there, in which she is accompanied by yours,

Wm Cowper

XIII *To William Unwin*   31 October 1779

My Dear Friend,

I wrote my last letter merely to inform you that I had nothing to say; in answer to which you have said nothing. I admire the propriety of your conduct though I am a loser by it. I will endeavour to say something now, and shall hope for something in return.

I have been well entertained with Johnson's biography, for which I thank you: with one exception, and that a swingeing one, I think he has acquitted himself with his usual good sense and sufficiency. His treatment of Milton is unmerciful to the last degree. A pensioner is not likely to spare a republican; and the Doctor, in order, I suppose, to convince his royal patron of the sincerity of his monarchical principles, has belaboured that great poet's character with the most industrious cruelty. As a man, he has hardly left him the shadow of one good quality. Churlishness in his private life, and a rancorous hatred of every-thing royal in his public, are the two colours with which he has smeared all the canvas. If he had any virtues, they are not to be

17

found in the Doctor's picture of him; and it is well for Milton, that some sourness in his temper is the only vice with which his memory has been charged; it is evident enough that if his biographer could have discovered more, he would not have spared him. As a poet, he has treated him with severity enough, and has plucked one or two of the most beautiful feathers out of his Muse's wing, and trampled them under his great foot. He has passed sentence of condemnation upon *Lycidas*, and has taken occasion, from that charming poem, to expose to ridicule, (what is indeed ridiculous enough,) the childish prattlement of pastoral compositions, as if *Lycidas* was the prototype and pattern of them all. The liveliness of the description, the sweetness of the numbers, the classical spirit of antiquity that prevails in it, go for nothing. I am convinced by the way, that he has no ear for poetical numbers, or that it was stopped by prejudice against the harmony of Milton's. Was there ever any thing so delightful as the music of the *Paradise Lost*? It is like that of a fine organ; has the fullest and the deepest tones of majesty, with all the softness and elegance of the Dorian flute. Variety without end and never equalled, unless perhaps by Virgil. Yet the Doctor has little or nothing to say upon this copious theme, but talks something about the unfitness of the English language for blank verse, and how apt it is, in the mouth of some readers, to degenerate into declamation. Oh! I could thresh his old jacket, till I made his pension jingle in his pocket.

I could talk a good while longer, but I have no room; our love attends you. – Yours affectionately,

W.C.

XIV *To William Unwin*   27 February 1780

Sir Joshua Reynolds (1723–92) was the leading portrait painter of the eighteenth century. He was also an influential art critic. Beginning in 1769, he gave a series of well attended annual lectures on art at the Royal Academy.

Edmund Burke (1729–97) was a renowned intellectual,

writer and Whig politician who eloquently defended the rights of people in the colonies, particularly Ireland and America. His vehement opposition to the French Revolution is most famously set out in his *Reflections on the Revolution in France*.

My Dear Friend,

As you are pleased to desire my letters, I am the more pleased with writing them; though at the same time I must needs testify my surprise that you should think them worth receiving, as I seldom send one that I think favourably of myself. This is not to be understood as an imputation upon your taste or judgment, but as an encomium upon my own modesty and humility, which I desire you to remark well. It is a just observation of Sir Joshua Reynolds, that though men of ordinary talents may be highly satisfied with their own productions, men of true genius never are. Whatever be their subject, they always seem to themselves to fall short of it, even when they seem to others most to excel. And for this reason, – because they have a certain sublime sense of perfection, which other men are strangers to, and which they themselves in their performances are not able to exemplify. Your servant, Sir Joshua! I little thought of seeing you when I began; but as you have popped in you are welcome.

When I wrote last, I was a little inclined to send you a copy of verses entitled the Modern Patriot, but was not quite pleased with a line or two, which I found it difficult to mend, therefore did not. At night I read Mr Burke's speech in the newspaper, and was so well pleased with his proposals for a reformation, and with the temper in which he made them, that I began to think better of his cause, and burnt my verses. Such is the lot of the man who writes upon the subject of the day; the aspect of affairs changes in an hour or two, and his opinion with it; what was just and well-deserved satire in the morning, in the evening becomes a libel; the author commences his own judge, and while he condemns with unrelenting severity what he so lately approved, is sorry to find that he has laid his leaf-gold upon touchwood, which crumbled away under his fingers. Alas! what can I do with my wit? I have not enough to do great things with, and these little things are so fugitive, that while a man catches at the subject, he is only filling his hand with smoke. I must do with it as I do with my linnet; I keep him for the most part in a cage, but now and then set open the door, that he may whisk about the room a little, and then shut him up again. [...]

Thanks for all you have done, and all you intend; the biography will be particularly welcome. – Yours,

W.C.

XV *To Mrs Newton*   4 March 1780

Newton left Olney in 1780 to take up the Rectorship of St Mary Woolnoth in London. He was replaced as curate by Benjamin Page.

Dear Madam,

To communicate surprise is almost, perhaps quite, as agreeable as to receive it. This is my present motive for writing to you rather than to Mr Newton. He would be pleased with hearing from me, but he would not be surprised at it; you see, therefore, I am selfish upon the present occasion, and principally consult my own gratification. Indeed, if I consulted yours, I should be silent, for I have no such budget as the minister's furnished and stuffed with ways and means for every emergency, and shall find it difficult, perhaps, to raise supplies even for a short epistle.

You have observed in common conversation, that the man who coughs and blows his nose the oftenest, (I mean if he has not a cold,) does it because he has nothing to say. Even so it is in letter-writing: a long preface, such as mine, is an ugly symptom, and always forebodes great sterility in the following pages.

The vicarage-house became a melancholy object, as soon as Mr Newton had left it; when you left it, it became more melancholy: now it is actually occupied by another family, even I cannot look at it without being shocked. As I walked in the

20

garden this evening, I saw the smoke issue from the study chimney, and said to myself, that used to be a sign that Mr Newton was there; but it is so no longer. The walls of the house know nothing of the change that has taken place; the bolt of the chamber-door sounds just as it used to do; and when Mr Page goes upstairs, for aught I know, or ever shall know, the fall of his foot could hardly, perhaps, be distinguished from that of Mr Newton. But Mr Newton's foot will never be heard upon that staircase again. These reflections, and such as these, occurred to me upon the occasion, and though in many respects I have no more sensibility left than there is in brick and mortar, yet I am not permitted to be quite unfeeling upon this subject. If I were in a condition to leave Olney too, I certainly would not stay in it. It is no attachment to the place that binds me here, but an unfitness for every other. I lived in it once, but now I am buried in it, and have no business with the world on the outside of my sepulchre; my appearance would startle them, and theirs would be shocking to me.

Such are my thoughts about the matter. Others are more deeply affected, and by more weighty considerations, having been many years the objects of a ministry which they had reason to account themselves happy in the possession of; they fear they shall find themselves great sufferers by the alteration that has taken place; they would have had reason to fear it in any case. But Mr Newton's successor does not bring with him the happiest presages, so that in the present state of things they have double reason for their fears. Though I can never be the better for Mr Page, Mr Page shall never be the worse for me. If his conduct should even justify the worst apprehensions that have been formed of his character, it is no personal concern of mine. But this I can venture to say, that if he is not spotless, his spots will be seen, and the plainer, because he comes after Mr Newton.

[...]

My respects attend Mr Newton and yourself, accompanied with much affection for you both. – Yours, dear Madam,

W.C.

Dear Sir,

You indulge me in such a variety of subjects, and allow me such a latitude of excursion in this scribbling employment, that I have no excuse for silence. I am much obliged to you for swallowing such boluses as I send you, for the sake of my gilding, and verily believe that I am the only man alive, from whom they would be welcome to a palate like yours. I wish I could make them more splendid than they are, more alluring to the eye, at least, if not more pleasing to the taste; but my leaf gold is tarnished, and has received such a tinge from the vapours that are ever brooding over my mind, that I think it no small proof of your partiality to me, that you will read my letters. I am not fond of longwinded metaphors; I have always observed, that they halt at the latter end of their progress, and so do mine. I deal much in ink indeed, but not such ink as is employed by poets, and writers of essays. Mine is a harmless fluid, and guilty of no deceptions but such as may prevail without the least injury to the person imposed on. I draw mountains, valleys, woods, and streams, and ducks, and dab-chicks. I admire them myself, and Mrs Unwin admires them; and her praise, and my praise put together, are fame enough for me. O! I could spend whole days and moonlight nights in feeding upon a lovely prospect! My eyes drink the rivers as they flow. If every human being upon earth could think for one quarter of an hour as I have done for many years, there might perhaps be many miserable men among them, but not an unawakened one could be found from the arctic to the antarctic circle. At present, the difference between them and me is greatly to their advantage. I delight in baubles, and know them to be so; for rested in, and viewed without a reference to their Author, what is the earth, – what are the planets, – what is the sun itself but a bauble? Better for a man never to have seen them, or to see them with the eyes of a brute, stupid and unconscious of what he beholds, than not to be able to say, ' The Maker of all these wonders is my friend!' Their eyes have never been opened, to see that they are trifles; mine have been, and will be till they are closed for ever. They think a fine estate, a large conservatory, a hothouse rich as a West Indian garden, things of consequence; visit them with pleasure, and muse upon them with ten times more. I am pleased with a frame of four lights, doubtful whether the few pines it contains will ever be worth a farthing; amuse myself with a greenhouse which Lord Bute's gardener could take upon his back, and walk away with; and when I have paid it the accustomed visit, and watered it, and given it air, I say to myself – 'This is not mine, it is a plaything lent me for the present; I must leave it soon.'

W.C.

XVII *To William Unwin*   8 May 1780

The Latin quotation in this letter is from Horace's *Satires*, and might be translated as 'Life give nothing to men without much labour'.

My Dear Friend,

My scribbling humour has of late been entirely absorbed in the passion for landscape drawing. It is a most amusing art, and like every other art, requires much practice and attention.

> *Nil sine multo*
> *Vita labore dedit mortalibus.*

Excellence is providentially placed beyond the reach of indolence, that success may be the reward of industry, and that idleness may be punished with obscurity and disgrace. So long as I am pleased with an employment, I am capable of unwearied application, because my feelings are all of the intense kind. I never received a *little* pleasure from any thing in my life; if I am delighted, it is in the extreme. The unhappy consequence of this temperature is, that my attachment to any occupation seldom outlives the novelty of it. That nerve of my imagination that feels the touch of any particular amusement, twangs under the energy of the pressure with so much vehemence, that it soon becomes sensible of weariness and fatigue. Hence I draw an unfavourable prognostic, and expect that I shall shortly be constrained to look out for something else. Then perhaps I may string the lyre again, and be able to comply with your demand.

Now for the visit you propose to pay us, and propose *not* to pay us; the hope of which plays about upon your paper, like a jack-o-lantern upon the ceiling. This is no mean simile, for Virgil (you remember) uses it. It is here, it is there, it vanishes, it returns, it dazzles you, a cloud interposes, and it is gone. However just the comparison, I hope you will contrive to spoil it, and that your final determination will be to come. As to the masons you expect, bring them with you; – bring brick, bring mortar, bring every thing that would oppose itself to your journey; – all shall be welcome. I have a greenhouse that is too small, come and enlarge it; build me a pinery; repair the garden wall, that has great need of your assistance; do any thing; you cannot do too much; so far from thinking you and your train troublesome, we shall rejoice to see you, upon these or upon any other terms you can propose. But to be serious, – you will do well to consider that a long summer is before you; that the party will not have such another opportunity to meet this great while; that you may finish your masonry long enough before winter, though you should not begin this month, but that you cannot always find your brother and sister Powley at Olney. These, and some other considerations, such as the desire we have to see you, and the pleasure we expect from seeing you all together, may, and, I think, ought to overcome your scruples.

[…] – Yours, my dear friend,

W.C.

XVIII *To Mrs Newton*   5 June 1780

Dear Madam,

When I write to Mr Newton, he answers me by letter; when I write to you, you answer me in fish. I return you many thanks for the mackerel and lobster. They assured me in terms as intelligible as pen and ink could have spoken, that you still remember *Orchardside*; and though they never spoke in their lives, and it was still less to be expected from them that they should speak, being dead, they gave us an assurance of your affection that corresponds exactly with that which Mr Newton expresses towards us in all his letters. – For my own part, I never in my life began a letter more at a venture than the present. It is possible that I may finish it, but perhaps more than probable that I shall not. I have had several indifferent nights, and the wind is easterly; two circumstances so unfavourable to me in all my occupations, but especially that of writing, that it was with the greatest difficulty I could even bring myself to attempt it.

You have never yet perhaps been made acquainted with the unfortunate Tom Freeman's misadventure. He and his wife returning from Hanslip fair, were coming down Weston Lane; to wit, themselves, their horse, and their great wooden panniers, at ten o'clock at night. The horse having a lively imagination, and very weak nerves, fancied he either saw or heard something, but has never been able to say what. A sudden fright will impart activity, and a momentary vigour, even to lameness itself. Accordingly, he started, and sprung from the middle of the road to the side of it, with such surprising alacrity, that he dismounted the gingerbread baker and his gingerbread wife in a moment. Not contented with this effort, nor thinking himself yet out of danger, he proceeded as fast as he could to a full gallop, rushed against the gate at the bottom of the lane, and opened it for himself, without perceiving that there was any gate there. Still he galloped, and with a velocity and momentum continually increasing, till he arrived in Olney. I had been in bed about ten minutes, when I heard the most uncommon and unaccountable noise that can be imagined. It was, in fact, occasioned by the clattering of tin pattypans and a Dutch-oven against the sides of the panniers. Much gingerbread was picked up in the street, and Mr Lucy's windows were broken all to pieces. Had this been all, it would have been a comedy, but we learned the next morning, that the poor woman's collar-bone was broken, and she has hardly been able to resume her occupation since.

[...] – Yours, dear Madam,

Wm. Cowper

XIX *To William Unwin*   8 June 1780

My Dear Friend,

It is possible I might have indulged myself in the pleasure of writing to you, without waiting for a letter from you, but for a reason which you will not easily guess. Your mother communicated to me the satisfaction you expressed in my correspondence, that you thought me entertaining and clever, and so forth: – now you must know, I love praise dearly, especially from the judicious, and those who have so much delicacy themselves as not to offend mine in giving it. But then, I found this consequence attending, or likely to attend the eulogium you bestowed; – if my friend thought me witty before, he shall think me ten times more witty hereafter; – where I joked once, I will joke five times, and for one sensible remark I will send him a dozen. Now this foolish vanity would have spoiled me quite, and would have made me as disgusting a letter-writer as Pope, who seems to have thought that unless a sentence was well turned, and every period pointed with some conceit, it was not worth the carriage. Accordingly he is to me, except in very few instances, the most disagreeable maker of epistles that ever I met with. I was willing, therefore, to wait till the impression your commendation had made upon the foolish part of me was worn off, that I might scribble away as usual, and write my uppermost thoughts, and those only.

[...]

Your mother sends her love to all, and mine comes jogging along by the side of it. – Yours,

                                                                                    W.C.

The 'danger' Cowper describes in this letter refers to the
Gordon Riots which resulted from a series of Protestant
demonstrations against the Catholic Relief Act of 1778 that
was designed to lift the ban on the teaching of Catholic
ideas in schools and to allow Catholics to purchase land
and property in Britain. The demonstrations culminated
in the delivery of a petition to the Houses of Parliament by
Lord George Gordon and days of civil disorder in the
capital. The Protestant Association was a group specifi-
cally formed to preserve the rights of Protestants at the
expense of Catholics.

Dear Sir,
    We accept it as an effort of your friendship, that you could
prevail with yourself, in a time of such terror and distress, to
send us repeated accounts of yours and Mrs Newton's welfare;
you supposed, with reason enough, that we should be apprehensive for your safety, situated as you were apparently within
the reach of so much danger. We rejoice that you have escaped
it all, and that, except the anxiety which you must have felt,
both for yourselves and others, you have suffered nothing upon
this dreadful occasion. A metropolis in flames, and a nation in
ruins, are subjects of contemplation for such a mind as yours
that will leave a lasting impression behind them. It is well that
the design died in the execution, and will be buried, I hope,
never to rise again, in the ashes of its own combustion. There is
a melancholy pleasure in looking back upon such a scene,
arising from a comparison of possibilities with facts, – the enormous bulk of the intended mischief, with the abortive and
partial accomplishment of it; much was done, more indeed than
could have been supposed practicable in a well regulated city,
not unfurnished with a military force for its protection. But
surprise and astonishment seem at first to have struck every
nerve of the police with a palsy, and to have disarmed government of all its powers.
    I congratulate you upon the wisdom that withheld you from

entering yourself a member of the Protestant Association. Your friends who did so, have reason enough to regret their doing it, even though they should never be called upon. Innocent as they are – and they who know them cannot doubt of their being perfectly so – it is likely to bring an odium on the profession they make, that will not soon be forgotten. Neither is it possible for a quiet, inoffensive man, to discover, on a sudden, that his zeal has carried him into such company, without being to the last degree shocked at his imprudence. Their religion was an honourable mantle, like that of Elijah; but the majority wore cloaks of Guy Fawkes's time, and meant nothing so little as what they pretended.

W.C.

XXI *To Joseph Hill*   8 July 1780

During the eighteenth century, Olney was one of the main centres of lace-making in England. At the time of this letter, a series of bills being put through Parliament, such as the removal of tariffs from Irish imports and a proposal to tax candles (in order to raise funds for Britain's war with America), looked set to put the already struggling workers even deeper into poverty.

Mon Ami,

If you ever take the tip of the Chancellor's ear between your finger and thumb, you can hardly improve the opportunity to better purpose, than if you should whisper into it the voice of compassion and lenity to the lace-makers. I am an eye-witness of their poverty, and do know that hundreds in this little town are upon the point of starving, and that the most unremitting industry is but barely sufficient to keep them from it. I know that the bill by which they would have been so fatally affected is thrown out: but Lord Stormont threatens them with another; and if another like it should pass, they are undone. We lately sent a petition to Lord Dartmouth; I signed it, and am sure the

28

contents are true. The purport of it was to inform him that there are very near one thousand two hundred lace-makers in this beggarly town, the most of whom had reason enough, while the bill was in agitation, to look upon every loaf they bought, as the last they should ever be able to earn. I can never think it good policy to incur the certain inconvenience of ruining thirty thousand, in order to prevent a remote and possible damage, though to a much greater number. The measure is like a scythe, and the poor lace-makers are the sickly crop that trembles before the edge of it. The prospect of a peace with America, is like the streak of dawn in their horizon; but this bill is like a black cloud behind it, that threatens their hope of a comfortable day with utter extinction.

I did not perceive till this moment, that I had tacked two similes together, – a practice which, though warranted by the example of Homer, and allowed in an epic poem, is rather luxuriant and licentious in a letter. Lest I should add another, I conclude.

W.C.

XXII *To William Unwin*   6 August 1780

My Dear Friend,

You like to hear from me: this is a very good reason why I should write. – But I have nothing to say: this seems equally a good reason why I should not. Yet if you had alighted from your horse at our door this morning, and at this present writing, being five o'clock in the afternoon, had found occasion to say to me – 'Mr Cowper, you have not spoke since I came in; have you resolved never to speak again?' it would be but a poor reply, if in answer to the summons I should plead inability as my best and only excuse. And this by the way suggests to me a seasonable piece of instruction, and reminds me of what I am very apt to forget, when I have any epistolary business in hand, that a letter may be written upon any thing or nothing just as that any thing or nothing happens to occur. A man that has a journey before him twenty miles in length, which he is to perform on foot, will not hesitate and doubt whether he shall set out or not, because he does not readily conceive how he shall ever reach the end of it: for he knows, that by the simple operation of moving one foot forward first, and then the other, he shall be sure to accomplish it. So it is in the present case, and so it is in every similar case. A letter is written as a conversation is maintained, or a journey performed; not by preconcerted or premeditated means, a new contrivance, or an invention never heard of before, – but merely by maintaining a progress, and resolving as a postilion does, having once set out, never to stop till we reach the appointed end. If a man may talk without thinking, why may he not write upon the same terms? A grave gentleman of the last century, a tie-wig, square-toe, Steinkirk figure, would say – 'My good sir, a man has no right to do either.' But it is to be hoped that the present century has nothing to do with the mouldy opinions of the last; and so good Sir Launcelot, or Sir Paul, or whatever be your name, step into your picture-frame again, and look as if you thought for another century, and leave us moderns in the mean time to think when we can, and to write whether we can or not, else we might as well be dead as you are.

When we look back upon our forefathers, we seem to look back upon the people of another nation, almost upon creatures of another species. Their vast rambling mansions, spacious halls, and painted casements, the gothic porch smothered with honeysuckles, their little gardens and high walls, their box-edgings, balls of holly, and yew-tree statues, are become so entirely unfashionable now, that we can hardly believe it possible, that a people who resembled us so little in their taste, should resemble us in any thing else. But in every thing else, I suppose, they were our counterparts exactly; and time, that has sewed up the slashed sleeve, and reduced the large trunk hose to a neat pair of silk stockings, has left human nature just where it found it. The inside of the man at least has undergone no change. His passions, appetites, and aims, are just what they ever were. They wear perhaps a handsomer disguise than they did in days of yore; for philosophy and literature will have their

30

effect upon the exterior; but in every other respect a modern is only an ancient in a different dress.

W.C.

XXIII *To John Newton*   21 August 1780

Cowper kept a wide range of pets throughout his life, from tame mice during his time in London to cats, spaniels and a bulldog. His most famous pets, however, were his three hares, Puss, Tiney and Bess, who became the subject of poems such as 'Epitaph on a Hare'. He describes them in detail in a letter to *The Gentleman's Magazine* in 1783 (see letter LIII), which also indicates his abhorrence at hunting animals for sport. In the third book of *The Task*, Cowper likens himself to a 'stricken deer' and, later, condemns the 'Detested sport, / That owes its pleasures to another's pain; / That feeds upon the sobs and dying shrieks / Of harmless nature'.

The Latin phrase at the end of this letter might be translated as, 'whatever affects me is of concern to you'.

The following occurrence ought not to be passed over in silence, in a place where so few notable ones are to be met with. Last Wednesday night, while we were at supper, between the hours of eight and nine, I heard an unusual noise in the back parlour, as if one of the hares was entangled, and endeavouring to disengage herself. I was just going to rise from table, when it ceased. In about five minutes, a voice on the outside of the parlour door inquired if one of my hares had got away. I immediately rushed into the next room, and found that my poor favourite Puss had made her escape. She had gnawed in sunder the strings of a lattice work, with which I thought I had sufficiently secured the window, and which I preferred to any other sort of blind, because it admitted plenty of air. From thence I hastened to the kitchen, where I saw the redoubtable Thomas Freeman, who told me, that having seen her, just after she had dropped into the street, he attempted to cover her with his hat, but she screamed out, and leaped directly over his head. I then desired him to pursue as fast as possible, and added Richard Coleman to the chase, as being nimbler, and carrying less weight than Thomas; not expecting to see her again, but desirous to learn, if possible, what became of her. In something less than an hour, Richard returned, almost breathless, with the following account. That soon after he began to run, he left Tom behind him, and came in sight of a most numerous hunt of men, women, children, and dogs; that he did his best to keep back the dogs, and presently outstripped the crowd, so that the race was at last disputed between himself and Puss; – she ran right through the town, and down the lane that leads to Dropshort; a little before she came to the house, he got the start and turned her; she pushed for the town again, and soon after she entered it, sought shelter in Mr Wagstaff's tanyard, adjoining to old Mr Drake's. Sturges's harvest men were at supper, and saw her from the opposite side of the way. There she encountered the tanpits full of water; and while she was struggling out of one pit, and plunging into another, and almost drowned, one of the men drew her out by the ears, and secured her. She was then well washed in a bucket, to get the lime out of her coat, and brought home in a sack at ten o'clock.

This frolic cost us four shillings, but you may believe we did not grudge a farthing of it. The poor creature received only a little hurt in one of her claws, and in one of her ears, and is now almost as well as ever.

I do not call this an answer to your letter, but such as it is I send it, presuming upon that interest which I know you take in my minutest concerns, which I cannot express better than in the words of Terence a little varied – *Nihil mei a te alienum putas*. – Yours, my dear friend,

W.C.

My Dear Friend,

I am glad you are so provident, and that, while you are yet young, you have furnished yourself with the means of comfort in old age. Your crutch and your pipe may be of use to you, (and may they be so,) should your years be extended to an antediluvian date; and for your present accommodation, you seem to want nothing but a clerk called Snuffle, and a sexton of the name of Skeleton, to make your ministerial equipage complete.

[...]

If you could meet with a second-hand Virgil, ditto Homer, both *Iliad* and *Odyssey*, together with a Clavis, for I have no Lexicon, and all tolerably cheap, I shall be obliged to you if you will make the purchase. – Yours,

W.C.

My Dear Friend,

Poetical reports of law cases are not very common, yet it seems to me desirable than they should be so. Many advantages would accrue from such a measure. They would in the first place be more commodiously deposited in the memory, just as linen, grocery, or other such matters, when neatly packed, are known to occupy less room, and to lie more conveniently in any trunk, chest, or box, to which they may be committed. In the next place, being divested of that infinite circumlocution, and the endless embarrassment in which they are involved by it, they would become surprisingly intelligible, in comparison with their present obscurity. And lastly, they would by this means be rendered susceptible of musical embellishment, and instead of being quoted in the courts, with that dull monotony, which is so wearisome to by-standers, and frequently lulls even the judges themselves to sleep, might be rehearsed in recitative; which would have an admirable effect, in keeping the attention fixed and lively, and could not fail to disperse that heavy atmosphere of sadness and gravity, which hangs over the jurisprudence of our country. I remember, many years ago, being informed by a relation of mine, who in his youth had applied himself to the study of the law, that one of his fellow students, a gentleman of sprightly parts, and very respectable talents of the poetical kind, did actually engage in the prosecution of such a design; for reasons I suppose somewhat similar to, if not the same with those I have now suggested. He began with Coke's *Institutes*; a book so rugged in its style, that an attempt to polish it seemed an Herculean labour, and not less arduous and difficult, than it would be to give the smoothness of a rabbit's fur to the prickly back of a hedgehog. But he succeeded to admiration, as you will perceive by the following specimen, which is all that my said relation could recollect of the performance.

Tenant in fee
Simple, is he,
And need neither quake nor quiver,
Who hath his lands,
Free from all demands
To him and his heirs for ever.

You have an ear for music, and a taste for verse, which saves me the trouble of pointing out with a critical nicety the advantages of such a version. [...]

W.C.

XXVI *To John Newton*   21 January 1781

In May 1779, after the publication of *Olney Hymns*, Cowper began work on a series of lyric poems that examine the moral state of England. Many of these were included in the collection, *Poems*, that was published in 1782. 'The Progress of Error' and 'Truth', referred to in this letter, are two of the eight substantial poems that make up the bulk of that collection. The others are 'Table Talk', 'Expostulation', 'Hope', 'Charity', 'Conversation' and 'Retirement'. *Poems* also contains thirty-four shorter poems that cover a wide range of subjects, often in a witty manner.

My Dear Sir,

I am glad that the *Progress of Error* did not Err in its Progress, as I feared it had; and that it has reached you safe; and still more pleased that it has met with your approbation; for if it had not, I should have wished it had miscarried, and have been sorry that the bearer's memory had served him so well upon the occasion. I knew him to be that sort of genius, which, being much busied in making excursions of the imaginary kind, is not always present to its own immediate concerns, much less to those of others; and having reposed the trust in him, began to regret that I had done so, when it was too late. But I did it to save a frank, and as the affair has turned out, that end was very well answered. This is committed to the hands of a less volatile person, and therefore more to be depended on.

As to the poem called *Truth*, which is already longer than its elder brother, and is yet to be lengthened by the addition of perhaps twenty lines, perhaps more; I shrink from the thought of transcribing it at present. But as there is no need to be in any hurry about it, I hope that in some rainy season, which the next month will probably bring with it, when perhaps I may be glad of employment, the undertaking will appear less formidable.

You need not withhold from us any intelligence relating to yourselves, upon an apprehension that Mr Raban has been beforehand with you upon those subjects, for he came down as costive as if you had fed him with nothing but quinces, and unless we engineered him with question after question, we could get nothing out of him. I have known such travellers in my time, and Mrs Newton is no stranger to one of them, who keep all their observations and discoveries to themselves, till they are extorted from them by mere dint of examination, and cross-examination. He told us indeed that some invisible agent supplied you every Sunday with a coach, which we were pleased with hearing; and this, I think, was the sum total of his information.

[...] – Yours, my dear friend,

Wm. Cowper

XXVII *To John Newton*   18 February 1781

My Dear Friend,

I send you *Table Talk*. It is a medley of many things, some that may be useful, and some that, for aught I know, may be very diverting. I am merry that I may decoy people into my company, and grave that they may be the better for it. Now and then I put on the garb of a philosopher, and take the opportunity that disguise procures me, to drop a word in favour of religion. In short, there is some froth, and here and there a bit of sweet-meat, which seems to entitle it justly to the name of a certain dish the ladies call a trifle. I did not choose to be more facetious, lest I should consult the taste of my readers at the expense of my own approbation; nor more serious than I have been, lest I should forfeit theirs. A poet in my circumstances has a difficult part to act: one minute obliged to bridle his humour, if he has any, and the next, to clap a spur to the sides of it: now ready to weep from a sense of the importance of his subject, and on a sudden constrained to laugh, lest his gravity should be mistaken for dulness. If this be not violent exercise for the mind, I know not what is; and if any man doubt it, let him try. Whether all this management and contrivance be necessary, I do not know, but am inclined to suspect that if my Muse was to go forth clad in Quaker colour, without one bit of riband to enliven her appearance, she might walk from one end of London to the other, as little noticed as if she were one of the sisterhood indeed.

[...]

You had been married thirty-one years last Monday. When you married I was eighteen years of age, and had just left Westminster school. At that time, I valued a man according to his proficiency and taste in classical literature, and had the meanest opinion of all other accomplishments unaccompanied by that. I lived to see the vanity of what I had made my pride, and in a few years found that there were other attainments which would carry a man more handsomely through life, than a mere knowledge of what Homer and Virgil had left behind them. In measure, as my attachment to these gentry wore off, I found a more welcome reception among those whose acquaintance it was more my interest to cultivate. But all this time was spent in painting a piece of wood, that had no life in it. At last I began to think *indeed*; I found myself in possession of many baubles, but not one grain of solidity in all my treasures. Then I learned the truth, and then I lost it; and there ends my history. I would no more than you wish to live such a life over again, but for one reason. He that is carried to execution, though through the roughest road, when he arrives at the destined spot, would be glad, notwithstanding the many jolts he met with, to repeat his journey. – Yours, my dear Sir, with our joint love,

W.C.

XXVIII *To John Newton*   5 March 1781

The Johnson referred to in this letter is Joseph Johnson, Cowper's publisher. Joseph Johnson was the leading radical and Unitarian publisher of the late eighteenth century. Other notable authors published by him include: William Blake, Maria Edgeworth, Thomas Malthus, Thomas Paine, Joseph Priestley, Mary Wollstonecraft and William Wordsworth.

My Dear Friend,
Since writing is become one of my principal amusements, and I have already produced so many verses on subjects that entitle them to a hope that they may possibly be useful, I should be sorry to suppress them entirely, or to publish them to no purpose, for want of that cheap ingredient, the name of the

author. If my name therefore will serve them in any degree, as a passport into the public notice, they are welcome to it; and Mr Johnson will, if he pleases, announce me to the world by the style and title of

WILLIAM COWPER, ESQ.
Of the Inner Temple.

If you are of my mind, I think *Table Talk* will be the best to begin with, as the subjects of it are perhaps more popular; and one would wish, at first setting out, to catch the public by the ear, and hold them by it as fast as possible, that they may be willing to hear one, on a second and a third occasion.

[...]

Olney has seen this day what it never saw before, and what will serve it to talk of, I suppose, for years to come. At eleven o'clock this morning, a party of soldiers entered the town, driving before them another party, who, after obstinately defending the bridge for some time, were obliged to quit it, and run. They ran in very good order, frequently faced about and fired, but were at last obliged to surrender prisoners of war. There has been much drumming and shouting, much scampering about in the dirt, but not an inch of lace made in the town, at least at the Silver End of it.

It is our joint request that you will not again leave us unwritten to for a fortnight. We are so like yourselves in this particular, that we cannot help ascribing so long a silence to the worst cause. The longer your letters the better, but a short one is better than none.

Mrs Unwin is pretty well, and adds the greetings of her love to mine. – Yours, my dear friend,

Wm. Cowper

XXIX *To William Unwin*   1 May 1781

Your mother says I *must* write, and *must* admits of no apology; I might otherwise plead, that I have nothing to say, that I am weary, that I am dull, that it would be more convenient therefore for you, as well as for myself, that I should let it alone; but all these pleas, and whatever pleas besides either disinclination, indolence, or necessity might suggest, are overruled, as they ought to be, the moment a lady adduces her irrefragable argument, *you must.* You have still however one comfort left, that what I must write, you may, or may not read, just as it shall please you; unless Lady Anne at your elbow should say, you *must* read it, and then like a true knight you will obey without looking out for a remedy.

[...]

In the press, and speedily will be published, in one volume octavo, price three shillings, *Poems*, by William Cowper, of the Inner Temple, Esq. You may suppose, by the size of the publication, that the greatest part of them have been long kept secret, because you yourself have never seen them: but the truth is, that they are most of them, except what you have in your possession, the produce of the last winter. Two-thirds of the compilation will be occupied by four pieces, the first of which sprung up in the month of December, and the last of them in the month of March. They contain, I suppose, in all, about two thousand and five hundred lines; are known, or to be known in due time, by the names of *Table Talk – The Progress of Error – Truth – Expostulation*. Mr Newton writes a Preface, and Johnson is the publisher. The principal, I may say the only reason why I never mentioned to you, till now, an affair which I am just going to make known to all the world, (if *that* Mr All-the-world should think it worth his knowing,) has been this; that till within these few days, I had not the honour to know it myself. This may seem strange, but it is true; for not knowing where to find underwriters who would choose to insure them; and not finding it convenient to a purse like mine, to run any hazard, even upon the credit of my own ingenuity, I was very much in doubt for some weeks, whether any bookseller would be willing to subject himself to an ambiguity, that might prove very expensive in case of a bad market. But Johnson has heroically set all peradventures at defiance, and takes the whole charge upon himself. So out I come. [...] My muse will lay

herself at your feet immediately on her first public appearance.
– Yours, my dear friend,

W. C.

My Dear Sir,

I am in the press, and it is in vain to deny it. But how myste-
rious is the conveyance of intelligence from one end to the other
of your great city! – Not many days since, except one man, and
he but a little taller than yourself, all London was ignorant of it;
for I do not suppose that the public prints have yet announced
this most agreeable tidings, the title-page, which is the basis of
the advertisement, having so lately reached the publisher: and
now it is known to you, who live at least two miles distant from
my confidant upon the occasion.

My labours are principally the production of the last winter;
all indeed, except a few of the minor pieces. When I can find no
other occupation, I think, and when I think, I am very apt to do
it in rhyme. Hence it comes to pass that the season of the year
which generally pinches off the flowers of poetry, unfolds mine,
such as they are, and crowns me with a winter garland. In this
respect therefore, I and my contemporary bards are by no
means upon a par. They write when the delightful influences
of fine weather, fine prospects, and a brisk motion of the animal
spirits, make poetry almost the language of nature; and I, when
icicles depend from all the leaves of the Parnassian laurel, and
when a reasonable man would as little expect to succeed in
verse, as to hear a blackbird whistle. This must be my apology
to you for whatever want of fire and animation you may
observe in what you will shortly have the perusal of. As to the
public, if they like me not, there is no remedy. A friend will
weigh and consider all disadvantages, and make as large
allowances as an author can wish, and larger perhaps than he
has any right to expect; but not so the world at large; whatever
they do not like, they will not by any apology be persuaded to

forgive, and it would be in vain to tell *them*, that I wrote my
verses in January, for they would immediately reply, 'Why did
not you write them in May?' A question that might puzzle a
wiser head than we poets are generally blessed with.

W. C.

XXXI *To William Unwin*   23 May 1781

My Dear Friend,

If a writer's friends have need of patience, how much more
the writer! Your desire to see my muse in public, and mine to
gratify you, must both suffer the mortification of delay. I
expected that my trumpeter would have informed the world by
this time of all that is needful for them to know upon such an
occasion; and that an advertising blast, blown through every
newspaper, would have said – 'The poet is coming!' – But man,
especially man that writes verse, is born to disappointments, as
surely as printers and booksellers are born to be the most dilatory and tedious of all creatures. The plain English of this
magnificent preamble is, that the season of publication is just
elapsed, that the town is going into the country every day, and
that my book cannot appear till they return, that is to say, not
till next winter.

This misfortune however comes not without its attendant
advantage; I shall now have, what I should not otherwise have
had, an opportunity to correct the press myself; no small advantage upon any occasion, but especially important, where poetry
is concerned! A single erratum may knock out the brains of a
whole passage, and that perhaps, which of all others the unfortunate poet is the most proud of. Add to this, that now and then
there is to be found in a printing-house a presumptuous inter-
meddler, who will fancy himself a poet too, and what is still
worse, a better than he that employs him. The consequence is,
that with cobbling, and tinkering, and patching on here and
there a shred of his own, he makes such a difference between
the original and the copy, that an author cannot know his own

work again. Now as I choose to be responsible for nobody's dulness but my own, I am a little comforted, when I reflect that it will be in my power to prevent all such impertinence; and yet not without your assistance. It will be quite necessary, that the correspondence between me and Johnson should be carried on without the expense of postage, because proof sheets would make double or treble letters, which expense, as in every instance it must occur twice, first when the packet is sent, and again when it is returned, would be rather inconvenient to me, who, as you perceive, am forced to live by my wits, and to him, who hopes to get a little matter no doubt by the same means. Half a dozen franks therefore to me, and *totidem* to him, will be singularly acceptable, if you can, without feeling it in any respect a trouble, procure them for me.

[…]

Since I began to write long poems, I seem to turn up my nose at the idea of a short one. I have lately entered upon one, which, if ever finished, cannot easily be comprised in much less than a thousand lines! But this must make part of a second publication, and be accompanied, in due time, by others not yet thought of; for it seems (which I did not know till the bookseller had occasion to tell me so) that single pieces stand no chance, and that nothing less than a volume will go down. You yourself afford me a proof of the certainty of this intelligence, by sending me franks which nothing less than a volume can fill. I have accordingly sent you one, but am obliged to add, that had the wind been in any other point of the compass, or, blowing as it does from the east, had it been less boisterous, you must have been contented with a much shorter letter, but the abridgement of every other occupation is very favourable to that of writing.

I am glad I did not expect to hear from you by this post, for the boy has lost the bag in which your letter must have been enclosed, – another reason for my prolixity! – Yours affectionately,

W.C.

After a witty discussion of the meaning of 'turning the other cheek', this letter introduces two characters who are central to Cowper's life story: Lady Austen and Mrs Throckmorton. Lady Ann Austen became a close friend of Cowper after her husband, Robert Austen, died, and moved to Olney in 1781. Although her relationship with Cowper was often rocky, she exerted a great influence on his work, suggesting he write both 'John Gilpin' and *The Task*. The Throckmortons, a distinguished Roman Catholic family who lived at Weston Underwood, also became close friends of the poet. In 1786, Cowper and Mrs Unwin moved into the Lodge at Weston Hall to be near them. For Cowper's fullest description of the family, see letter LII.

My Dear Friend,

Having given the case you laid before me in your last all due consideration, I proceed to answer it; and in order to clear my way, shall, in the first place, set down my sense of those passages in Scripture which, on a hasty perusal, seem to clash with the opinion I am going to give – 'If a man smite one cheek, turn the other' – 'If he take thy cloak, let him take thy coat also.' That is, I suppose, rather than on a vindictive principle avail yourself of that remedy the law allows you, in the way of retaliation, for that was the subject immediately under the discussion of the speaker. Nothing is so contrary to the genius of the Gospel, as the gratification of resentment and revenge; but I cannot easily persuade myself to think, that the author of that dispensation could possibly advise his followers to consult their own peace at the expense of the peace of society, or inculcate a universal abstinence from the use of lawful remedies, to the encouragement of injury and oppression.

St Paul again seems to condemn the practice of going to law, 'Why do ye not rather suffer wrong?' &c. But if we look again, we shall find that a litigious temper had obtained, and was prevalent among the professors of the day. This he condemned, and with good reason; it was unseemly to the last degree, that the disciples of the Prince of Peace should worry and vex each other with injurious treatment, and unnecessary disputes, to the scandal of their religion in the eyes of the heathen. But surely he did not mean any more than his Master, in the place above alluded to, that the most harmless members of society should receive no advantage of its laws, or should be the only persons in the world who should derive no benefit from those institutions, without which society cannot subsist. Neither of them could mean to throw down the pale of property, and to lay the Christian part of the world open, throughout all ages, to the incursions of unlimited violence and wrong.

By this time you are sufficiently aware, that I think you have an indisputable right to recover at law what is so dishonestly withheld from you. The fellow, I suppose, has discernment enough to see a difference between you and the generality of the clergy, and cunning enough to conceive the purpose of turning your meekness and forbearance to good account, and of coining them into hard cash, which he means to put in his pocket. But I would disappoint him, and show him, that though a Christian is not to be quarrelsome, he is not to be crushed; and that though he is but a worm before God, he is not such a worm as every selfish unprincipled wretch may tread upon at his pleasure.

I lately heard a story from a lady, who has spent many years of her life in France, somewhat to the present purpose. An Abbé, universally esteemed for his piety, and especially for the meekness of his manners, had yet undesignedly given some offence to a shabby fellow in his parish. The man, concluding he might do as he pleased with so forgiving and gentle a character, struck him on one cheek, and bade him turn the other. The good man did so, and when he had received the two slaps, which he thought himself obliged to submit to, turned again, and beat him soundly. I do not wish to see you follow the French gentleman's example, but I believe nobody that has heard the story condemns him much for the spirit he showed upon the occasion.

I had the relation from Lady Austen, sister to Mrs Jones, wife of the minister at Clifton. She is a most agreeable woman, and has fallen in love with your mother and me; insomuch, that I do not know but she may settle at Olney. Yesterday se'nnight we all dined together in the *Spinnie* – a most delightful retirement, belonging to Mrs Throckmorton of Weston. Lady Austen's lackey, and a lad that waits on me in the garden, drove a wheelbarrow full of eatables and drinkables to the scene of our *Fête Champêtre*. A board laid over the top of the wheelbarrow served us for a table; our dining-room was a root-house lined with moss and ivy. At six o'clock, the servants, who had dined under a great elm upon the ground, at a little distance, boiled the kettle, and the said wheelbarrow served us for a tea-table. We then took a walk into the wilderness, about half a mile off, and were at home again a little after eight, having spent the day together from noon till evening without one cross occurrence, or the least weariness of each other. A happiness few parties of pleasure can boast of. – Yours, with our joint love,

W.C.

XXXIII *To William Unwin*   25 August 1781

My Dear Friend,

We rejoice with you sincerely in the birth of another son, and in the prospect you have of Mrs Unwin's recovery; may your three children, and the next three, when they shall make their appearance, prove so many blessings to their parents, and make you wish that you had twice the number. But what made you expect daily that you should hear from me? Letter for letter is the law of all correspondence whatsoever, and because I wrote last, I have indulged myself for some time in expectation of a sheet from you. Not that I govern myself entirely by the punctilio of reciprocation, but having been pretty much occupied of late, I was not sorry to find myself at liberty to exercise my discretion, and furnished with a good excuse if I chose to be silent.

I expected, as you remember, to have been published last

spring, and was disappointed. The delay has afforded me an opportunity to increase the quantity of my publication by about a third; and if my muse has not forsaken me, which I rather suspect to be the case, may possibly yet add to it. I have a subject in hand, which promises me a great abundance of poetical matter, but which, for want of a something I am not able to describe, I cannot at present proceed with. The name of it is 'Retirement,' and my purpose, to recommend the proper improvement of it, to set forth the requisites for that end, and to enlarge upon the happiness of that state of life, when managed as it ought to be. In the course of my journey through this ample theme, I should wish to touch upon the characters, the deficiencies, and the mistakes of thousands, who enter on a scene of retirement, unqualified for it in every respect, and with such designs as have no tendency to promote either their own happiness or that of others. But as I have told you before, there are times when I am no more a poet than I am a mathematician; and when such a time occurs, I always think it better to give up the point, than to labour it in vain. I shall yet again be obliged to trouble you for franks; the addition of three thousand lines, or near that number, having occasioned a demand which I did not always foresee: but your obliging friend, and your obliging self, having allowed me the liberty of application, I make it without apology.

The solitude, or rather the duality of our condition at Olney, seems drawing to a conclusion. You have not forgot, perhaps, that the building we inhabit consists of two mansions. And because you have only seen the inside of that part of it which is in our occupation, I therefore inform you, that the other end of it is by far the most superb, as well as the most commodious. Lady Austen has seen it, has set her heart upon it, is going to fit it up and furnish it, and if she can get rid of the remaining two years of the lease of her London house, will probably enter upon it in a twelvemonth. You will be pleased with this intelligence, because I have already told you, that she is a woman perfectly well bred, sensible, and in every respect agreeable; and above all, because she loves your mother dearly. It has in my eyes, (and I doubt not it will have the same in yours,) strong marks of providential interposition. A female friend, and one who bids fair to prove herself worthy of the appellation, comes, recommended by a variety of considerations, to such a place as Olney. Since Mr Newton went, and till this lady came, there was not in the kingdom a retirement more absolutely such than ours. We did not want company, but when it came, we found it agreeable. A person that has seen much of the world, and understands it well, has high spirits, a lively fancy, and great readiness of conversation, introduces a sprightliness into such a scene as this, which, if it was peaceful before, is not the worse for being a little enlivened. In case of illness too, to which all are liable, it was rather a gloomy prospect, if we allowed ourselves to advert to it, that there was hardly a woman in the place from whom it would have been reasonable to have expected either comfort or assistance. The present curate's wife is a valuable person, but has a family of her own, and though a neighbour, is not a very near one. But if this plan is effected, we shall be in a manner one family, and I suppose never pass a day without some intercourse with each other.

Your mother sends her warm affections, and welcomes into the world the new-born William. – Yours, my dear friend,

W.C.

XXXIV *To John Newton*   18 September 1781

Cowper arranged for John Newton to write an introduction to his *Poems*. This was later suppressed at the instigation of his publisher, Joseph Johnson. The Dr Watts of this letter is Isaac Watts (1674–1748), a religious nonconformist and one of the most popular poets of the early eighteenth century.

My Dear Friend,

I return your preface, with many thanks for so affectionate an introduction to the public. I have observed nothing that in my judgement required alteration, except a single sentence in the first paragraph, which I have not obliterated, that you may restore it if you please, by obliterating my interlineation. My reason for proposing an amendment of it was, that your meaning did not strike me, which therefore I have endeavoured to make more obvious. The rest is what I would wish it to be. You say, indeed, more in my commendation, than I can modestly say of myself: but something will be allowed to the partiality of friendship, on so interesting an occasion.

I have no objection in the world to your conveying a copy to Dr Johnson; though I well know that one of his pointed sarcasms, if he should happen to be displeased, would soon find its way into all companies, and spoil the sale. He writes, indeed, like a man that thinks a great deal, and that sometimes thinks religiously: but report informs me that he has been severe enough in his animadversions upon Dr Watts, who was nevertheless, if I am in any degree a judge of verse, a man of true poetical ability; careless, indeed, for the most part, and inattentive too often to those niceties which constitute elegance of expression, but frequently sublime in his conceptions, and masterly in his execution. Pope, I have heard, had placed him once in the *Dunciad*; but on being advised to read before he judged him, was convinced that he deserved other treatment, and thrust somebody's blockhead into the gap, whose name, consisting of a monosyllable, happened to fit it. Whatever faults, however, I may be chargeable with as a poet, I cannot accuse myself of negligence. I never suffer a line to pass till I have made it as good as I can; and though my doctrines may offend this king of critics, he will not, I flatter myself, be disgusted by slovenly inaccuracy, either in the numbers, rhymes, or language. Let the rest take its chance. It is possible he may be pleased; and if he should, I shall have engaged on my side one of the best trumpeters in the kingdom. Let him only speak as favourably of me as he has spoken of Sir Richard Blackmore (who, though he shines in his poem called *Creation*, has written more absurdities in verse than any writer of our country), and my success will be secured.

I have often promised myself a laugh with you about your pipe, but have always forgotten it when I have been writing, and at present I am not much in a laughing humour. You will observe, however, for your comfort and the honour of that same pipe, that it hardly falls within the line of my censure. You never fumigate the ladies, or force them out of company; nor do you use it as an incentive to hard drinking. Your friends, indeed, have reason to complain that it frequently deprives them of the pleasure of your own conversation while it leads you either into your study or your garden; but in all other respects it is as innocent a pipe as can be. Smoke away, therefore; and remember that if one poet has condemned the practice, a better than he (the witty and elegant Hawkins Browne,) has been warm in the praise of it.

Retirement grows, but more slowly than any of its predecessors. Time was when I could with ease produce fifty, sixty, or seventy lines in a morning: now, I generally fall short of thirty, and am sometimes forced to be content with a dozen. It consists at present, I suppose, of between six and seven hundred; so that there are hopes of an end, and I dare say Johnson will give me time enough to finish it.

I nothing add but this – that *still I am*
Your most affectionate and humble

WILLIAM

XXXV *To John Newton*   4 December 1781

My Dear Friend,
    The present to the Queen of France, and the piece addressed to Sir Joshua Reynolds, my only two political efforts, being of the predictive kind, and both falsified, or likely to be so, by the miscarriage of the royal cause in America, were already condemned when I received your last. I have a poetical epistle which I wrote last summer, and another poem not yet finished, in stanzas, with which I mean to supply their places. Henceforth I have done with politics. The stage of national affairs is such a fluctuating scene, that an event which appears probable today

becomes impossible tomorrow; and unless a man were indeed a prophet, he cannot, but with the greatest hazard of losing his labour, bestow his rhymes upon future contingencies, which perhaps are never to take place but in his own wishes and in the reveries of his own fancy. I learned when I was a boy, being the son of a staunch Whig, and a man that loved his country, to glow with that patriotic enthusiasm which is apt to break forth into poetry, or at least to prompt a person, if he has any inclination that way, to poetical endeavours. Prior's pieces of that sort were recommended to my particular notice; and as that part of the present century was a season when clubs of a political character, and consequently political songs, were much in fashion, the best in that style, some written by Rowe, and I think some by Congreve, and many by other wits of the day, were proposed to my admiration. Being grown up, I became desirous of imitating such bright examples, and while I lived in the Temple produced several halfpenny ballads, two or three of which had the honour to be popular. What we learn in childhood we retain long; and the successes we met with, about three years ago, when D'Estaing was twice repulsed, once in America, and once in the West Indies, having set fire to my patriotic zeal once more, it discovered itself by the same symptoms, and produced effects much like those it had produced before. But, unhappily, the ardour I felt upon the occasion, disdaining to be confined within the bounds of fact, pushed me upon uniting the prophetical with the poetical character, and defeated its own purpose. I am glad it did. The less there is of that sort in my book the better; it will be more consonant to your character, who patronise the volume, and, indeed, to the constant tenor of my own thoughts upon public matters, that I should exhort my countrymen to repentance, than that I should flatter their pride – that vice for which, perhaps, they are even now so severely punished.

[...]

Easterly winds, and a state of confinement within our own walls, suit neither me nor Mrs Unwin; though we are both, to use the Irish term, rather unwell than ill. The cocoa nut though it had not a drop of liquor in it, and though the kernel came out whole, entirely detached from the shell, was an exceeding good one. Our hearts are with you. – Yours, my dear friend,

W.C.

[…]

XXXVI *To Joseph Hill*   9 December 1781

My Dear Friend,

Having returned you many thanks for the fine cod and oysters you favoured me with, though it is now morning I will suppose it afternoon, that you and I dined together, are comfortably situated by a good fire, and just entering on a sociable conversation. You speak first, because I am a man of few words.

Well, Cowper, what do you think of this American war?

I. To say the truth I am not very fond of thinking about it; when I do I think of it, unpleasantly enough. I think it bids fair to be the ruin of the country.

You. That's very unpleasant indeed! If that should be the consequence, it will be the fault of those who might put a stop to it if they would.

I. But do you really think that practicable?

You. Why not? If people leave off fighting, peace follows of course. I wish they would withdraw the forces and put an end to the squabble.

Now I am going to make a long speech.

I. You know the complexion of my sentiments upon some subjects well enough, and that I do not look upon public events either as fortuitous, or absolutely derivable either from the wisdom or folly of man. These indeed operate as second causes; but we must look for the cause of the decline or the prosperity of an empire elsewhere. I have long since done complaining of men and measures, having learned to consider them merely as the instruments of a higher Power, by which he either bestows wealth, peace, and dignity upon a nation when he favours it; or by which he strips it of all those honours, when public enormities long persisted in provoke him to inflict a public

51

punishment. The counsels of great men become as foolish and preposterous when he is pleased to make them so, as those of the frantic creatures in Bedlam, when they lay their distracted heads together to consider of the state of the nation. But I go still farther. The wisdom, or the want of wisdom, that we observe or think we observe in those that rule us, entirely out of the question, I cannot look upon the circumstances of this country, without being persuaded that I discern in them an entanglement and perplexity that I have never met with in the history of any other, which I think preternatural (if I may use the word on such a subject), prodigious in its kind, and such as human sagacity can never remedy. I have a good opinion of the understanding and integrity of some in power, yet I see plainly that they are unequal to the task. I think as favourably of some that are not in power, yet I am sure they have never yet in any of their speeches recommended the plan that would effect the salutary purpose. If we pursue the war, it is because we are desperate; it is plunging and sinking year after year into still greater depths of calamity. If we relinquish it, the remedy is equally desperate, and would prove I believe in the end no remedy at all. Either way we are undone. Perseverance will only enfeeble us more; we cannot recover the colonies by arms. If we discontinue the attempt, in that case we fling away voluntarily what in the other we strive ineffectually to regain; and whether we adopt the one measure or the other, are equally undone: for I consider the loss of America as the ruin of England. Were we less encumbered than we are at home, we could but ill afford it; but being crushed as we are under an enormous debt that the public credit can at no rate carry much longer, the consequence is sure. Thus it appears to me that we are squeezed to death, between the two sides of that sort of alternative which is commonly called a cleft stick, the most threatening and portentous condition in which the interests of any country can possibly be found.

I think I have done pretty well for a man of few words, and have contrived to have all the talk to myself. I thank you for not interrupting me. – Yours, my dear friend,

Wm. Cowper

Confusingly, perhaps, the 'Johnson' of this letter is Joseph
Johnson, and the 'critical Doctor' is Samuel Johnson.

My Dear Friend,
   [...]
   I thank you for the jog you gave Johnson's elbow; communicated from him to the printer, it has produced me two more
sheets, and two more will bring the business, I suppose, to a
conclusion. I sometimes feel such a perfect indifference with
respect to the public opinion of my book, that I am ready to
flatter myself no censure of reviewers, or other critical readers,
would occasion me the smallest disturbance. But not feeling
myself constantly possessed of this desirable apathy, I am
sometimes apt to suspect, that it is not altogether sincere, or at
least that I may lose just in the moment when I may happen
most to want it. Be it, however, as it may, I am still persuaded
that it is not in their power to mortify me much. I have intended
well, and performed to the best of my ability – so far was right,
and this is a boast of which they cannot rob me. If they condemn
my poetry, I must even say with Cervantes, 'Let them do better
if they can!' – if my doctrine, they judge that which they do not
understand; I shall except to the jurisdiction of the court, and
plead, *Coram non judice*. Even Horace could say, he should
neither be the plumper for the praise, nor the leaner for the
condemnation of his readers; and it will prove me wanting to
myself indeed, if, supported by so many sublimer considerations than he was master of, I cannot sit loose to popularity,
which, like the wind, bloweth where it listeth, and is equally
out of our command. [...]
   I am rather pleased that you have adopted other sentiments
respecting our intended present to the critical Doctor. I allow
him to be a man of gigantic talents, and most profound learning,
nor have I any doubts about the universality of his knowledge.
But by what I have seen of his animadversions on the poets, I
feel myself much disposed to question, in many instances,
either his candour or his taste. He finds fault too often, like a

man that, having sought it very industriously, is at last obliged to stick it on a pin's point, and look at it through a microscope; and I am sure I could easily convict him of having denied many beauties, and overlooked more. Whether his judgment be in itself defective, or whether it be warped by collateral considerations, a writer upon such subjects as I have chosen would probably find but little mercy at his hands.

No winter since we knew Olney has kept us more confined than the present. We have not more than three times escaped into the fields since last autumn. Man, a changeable creature in himself, seems to subsist best in a state of variety, as his proper element – a melancholy man, at least, is apt to grow sadly weary of the same walks, and the same pales, and to find that the same scene will suggest the same thoughts perpetually.

Though I have spoken of the utility of changes, we neither feel nor wish for any in our friendships, and consequently stand just where we did in respect to your whole self. – Yours, my dear sir,

W.C.

XXXVIII *To William Unwin*   9 February 1782

The 'lady...in Queen Anne Street' is Lady Austen.

My Dear Friend,

[...]

I have a piece of secret history to communicate which I would have imparted sooner, but that I thought it possible there might be no occasion to mention it at all. When persons for whom I have felt a friendship, disappoint and mortify me by their conduct, or act unjustly towards me, though I no longer esteem them friends, I still feel that tenderness for their character that I would conceal the blemish if I could. But in making known the following anecdote to you, I run no risk of a publication, assured that when I have once enjoined your secrecy, you will observe it.

My letters have already apprized you of that close and intimate connexion that took place between the lady you visited in Queen Ann Street, and us. Nothing could be more promising, though sudden in the commencement. She treated us with as much unreservedness of communication, as if we had been born in the same house, and educated together. At her departure, she herself proposed a correspondence, and because writing does not agree with your mother, proposed a correspondence with me. This sort of intercourse had not been long maintained, before I discovered, by some slight intimations of it, that she had conceived displeasure at somewhat I had written, though I cannot now recollect it: conscious of none but the most upright inoffensive intentions, I yet apologized for the passage in question, and the flaw was healed again. Our correspondence after this proceeded smoothly for a considerable time, but at length having had repeated occasion to observe that she expressed a sort of romantic idea of our merits, and built such expectations of felicity upon our friendship, as we were sure that nothing human could possibly answer, I wrote to remind her that we were mortal, to recommend it to her not to think more highly of us than the subject would warrant, and intimating that when we embellish a creature with colours taken from our own fancy, and so adorned, admire and praise it beyond its real merits, we make it an idol, and have nothing to expect in the end, but that it will deceive our hopes, and that we shall derive nothing from it but a painful conviction of our error. Your mother heard me read the letter, she read it herself, and honoured it with her warm approbation. But it gave mortal offence; it received indeed an answer, but such an one as I could by no means reply to; and there ended (for it was impossible it should ever be renewed) a friendship that bid fair to be lasting; being formed with a woman whose seeming stability of temper, whose knowledge of the world, and great experience of its folly, but above all, whose sense of religion, and seriousness of mind, (for with all that gaiety, she is a great thinker,) induced us both, in spite of that cautious reserve that marks our characters, to trust her, to love and value her, and to open our hearts for her reception. It may be necessary to add, that by her own desire I wrote to her under the assumed relation of a brother, and she to me as my sister.

[...] – Yours, my dear friend,

W.C.

XXXIX *To William Unwin* 18 March 1782

After long delays, *Poems* was finally published on 1 March 1782.

My Dear Friend,

Nothing has given me so much pleasure, since the publication of my volume, as your favourable opinion of it. It may possibly meet with acceptance from hundreds, whose commendation would afford me no other satisfaction than what I should find in the hope that it might do them good. I have some neighbours in this place, who say they like it; – doubtless I had rather they should than that they should not, – but I know them to be persons of no more taste in poetry, than skill in the mathematics; their applause therefore is a sound that has no music in it for me. But my vanity was not so entirely quiescent when I read your friendly account of the manner in which it had affected *you*. It was tickled, and pleased, and told me in a pretty loud whisper, that others perhaps of whose taste and judgement I had a high opinion, would approve it too. As a giver of good counsel, I wish to please all; – as an author, I am perfectly indifferent to the judgement of all, except the few who are indeed judicious. The circumstance however in your letter which pleased me the most was, that you wrote in high spirits, and though you said much, suppressed more, lest you should hurt my delicacy; my delicacy is obliged to you, – but you observe it is not so squeamish, but that after it has feasted upon praise expressed, it can find a comfortable dessert in the contemplation of praise implied. I now feel as if I should be glad to begin another volume, but from the will to the power is a step too wide for me to take at present, and the season of the year brings with it so many avocations into the garden, where I am my own *fac totum*, that I have little or no leisure for the quill. I should do myself much wrong, were I to omit mentioning the great complacency with which I read your narrative of Mrs Unwin's smiles and tears; persons of much sensibility are always persons of taste; a taste for poetry depends indeed upon that very article more than upon any other. If she had Aristotle by heart, I should not esteem her judgement so highly, were she defective in point of feeling, as I do and must esteem it, knowing her to have such feelings as Aristotle could not communicate, and as half the readers in the world are destitute of. This it is that makes me set so high a price upon your mother's opinion. She is a critic by nature, and not by rule, and has a perception of what is good or bad in composition, that I never knew deceive her; insomuch, that when two sorts of expression have pleaded equally for the preference, in my own esteem, and I have referred, as in such cases I always did, the decision of the point to her, I never knew her at a loss for a just one.

[…] – Yours ever,

W.C.

XL *To William Unwin*   27 May 1782

Benjamin Franklin, one of the leading politicians, writers and intellectuals of the period, was in France from 1779 until 1785, working as the American Plenipotentiary Minister to the Court of Versailles.

My Dear Friend,

Rather ashamed of having been at all dejected by the censure of the Critical Reviewers, who certainly could not read without prejudice a book replete with opinions and doctrines to which they cannot subscribe, I have at present no little occasion to keep a strict guard upon my vanity, lest it should be too much flattered by the following eulogium. I send it you for the reasons I gave when I imparted to you some other anecdotes of a similar kind, while we were together. Our interests in the success of this same volume are so closely united, that you *must* share with me in the praise or blame that attends it; and sympathising with me under the burthen of injurious treatment, have a right to enjoy with me the cordials I now and then receive, as I happen to meet with more favourable and candid judges.

A merchant, a friend of ours, (you will soon guess him,) sent my *Poems* to one of the first philosophers, one of the most eminent literary characters, as well as one of the most important in the political world, that the present age can boast of. Now perhaps your conjecturing faculties are puzzled, and you begin to ask, 'who, where, and what is he? speak out, for I am all impatience.' I will not say a word more, the letter in which he returned his thanks for the present shall speak for him.

Passy, 8 May 1782

Sir,

I received the letter you did me the honour of writing to me, and am much obliged by your kind present of a book. The relish for reading of poetry had long since left me, but there is something so new in the manner, so easy, and yet so correct in the language, so clear in the expression, yet concise, and so just in the sentiments, that I have read the whole with great pleasure, and some of the pieces more than once. I beg you to accept my thankful acknowledgements, and to present my respects to the author.

I shall take care to forward the letters to America, and shall be glad of any other opportunity of doing what may be agreeable to you, being with great respect for your character, –Your most obedient humble servant,

B. Franklin

We may now treat the critics as the Archbishop of Toledo treated Gil Blas, when he found fault with one of his sermons. His grace gave him a kick, and said, 'Begone for a jackanapes, and furnish yourself with a better taste, if you know where to find it.'

[…] Yours,

W.C.

After their falling out (see letter XXXVIII), Lady Austen began to make overtures towards a reconciliation. Cowper's response eventually persuaded her to move back to Olney.

To watch the storms, and hear the sky
Give all our almanacks the lie
To shake with cold, and see the plains
In autumn drown'd with wintry rains
'Tis thus I spend my moments here,
And wish myself a Dutch Mynheer;
I then should have no need of wit,
For lumpish Hollander unfit.
Nor should I then repine at mud,
Or meadows deluged with a flood;
But in a bog live well content,
And find it just my element;
Should be a clod, and not a man,
Nor wish in vain for Sister Ann,
With charitable aid to drag
My mind out of its proper quag;
Should have the genius of a boor,
And no ambition to have more.

My Dear Sister,

You see my beginning. I do not know but in time I may proceed even to the printing of halfpenny ballads – Excuse the coarseness of my paper; I wasted such a quantity before I could accomplish any thing legible, that I could not afford finer. I intend to employ an ingenious mechanic of the town to make me a longer case; for you may observe that my lines turn up their tails like Dutch mastiffs, so difficult do I find it to make the two halves exactly coincide with each other.

We wait with impatience for the departure of this unseasonable flood. We think of you, and talk of you, but we can do no more, till the waters shall subside. I do not think our correspondence should drop because we are within a mile of each other. It is but an imaginary approximation, the flood having in reality as effectually parted us as if the British Channel rolled between us. – Yours, my dear sister, with Mrs Unwin's best love.

W.C.

XLII *To William Unwin*   18 November 1782

Cowper's comic poem, 'The Diverting History of John Gilpin', which was suggested by an anecdote of Lady Austen's, first appeared anonymously in *The Public Advertiser* of 14 November 1782. It was published under Cowper's name as an appendix to *The Task* in 1785. The 'certain book' referred to in the final paragraph is, of course, Cowper's *Poems*.

My Dear William,
  [...]
I little thought when I was writing the history of John Gilpin, that he would appear in print – I intended to laugh, and to make two or three others laugh, of whom you were one. But now all the world laughs, at least if they have the same relish for a tale ridiculous in itself, and quaintly told, as we have. – Well – they do not always laugh so innocently, or at so small an expense – for in a world like this, abounding with subjects for satire, and with satirical wits to mark them, a laugh that hurts nobody has at least the grace of novelty to recommend it. Swift's darling motto was, *Vive la bagatelle* – a good wish for a philosopher of his complexion, the greater part of whose wisdom, whencesoever it came, most certainly came not from above. *La bagatelle* has no enemy in me, though it has neither so warm a friend, nor so able a one, as it had in him. If I trifle, and merely trifle, it is because I am reduced to it by necessity – a melancholy, that nothing else so effectually disperses, engages me sometimes in the arduous task of being merry by force. And, strange as it may

seem, the most ludicrous lines I ever wrote have been written in the saddest mood, and, but for that saddest mood, perhaps had never been written at all. To say truth, it would be but a shocking vagary, should the mariners on board a ship buffeted by a terrible storm, employ themselves in fiddling and dancing; yet sometimes much such a part act I.

I hear from Mrs Newton, that some great persons have spoken with great approbation of a certain book. – Who they are, and what they have said, I am to be told in a future letter. The Monthly Reviewers in the mean time have satisfied me well enough. – Yours, my dear William,

W.C.

XLIII *To Joseph Hill*   7 December 1782

My Dear Friend,

At seven o'clock this evening, being the seventh of December, I imagine I see you in your box at the coffee-house. No doubt the waiter, as ingenious and adroit as his predecessors were before him, raises the teapot to the ceiling with his right hand, while in his left the teacup descending almost to the floor, receives a limpid stream; limpid in its descent, but no sooner has it reached its destination, than frothing and foaming to the view, it becomes a roaring syllabub. This is the nineteenth winter since I saw you in this situation; and if nineteen more pass over me before I die, I shall still remember a circumstance we have often laughed at.

How different is the complexion of your evenings and mine! – yours, spent amid the ceaseless hum that proceeds from the inside of fifty noisy and busy periwigs; mine, by a domestic fireside, in a retreat as silent as retirement can make it; where no noise is made but what we make for our own amusement. For instance, here are two rustics, and your humble servant in company. One of the ladies has been playing on the harpsichord, while I, with the other, have been playing at battledore and shuttlecock. A little dog, in the mean time, howling under the chair of the former, performed, in the vocal way, to admiration. This entertainment over, I began my letter, and having nothing more important to communicate, have given you an account of it. I know you love dearly to be idle, when you can find an opportunity to be so; but as such opportunities are rare with you, I thought it possible that a short description of the idleness I enjoy might give you pleasure. The happiness we cannot call our own, we yet seem to possess, while we sympathise with our friends who can.

The papers tell me that peace is at hand, and that it is at a great distance; that the siege of Gibraltar is abandoned, and that it is to be still continued. It is happy for me, that though I love my country, I have but little curiosity. There was a time when these contradictions would have distressed me, but I have learnt by experience that it is best for little people like myself to be patient, and to wait till time affords the intelligence which no speculations of theirs can ever furnish.

I thank you for a fine cod with oysters, and hope that ere long, I shall have to thank you for procuring me Elliott's medicines. Every time I feel the least uneasiness in either eye, I tremble lest, my Æsculapius being departed, my infallible remedy should be lost for ever. Adieu. My respects to Mrs Hill. – Yours faithfully,

Wm. Cowper

XLIV *To John Newton*   8 February 1783

On 20 January 1783, the treaty of Paris was signed in which Britain acknowledged the conclusion of the war and the independence of America.

My Dear Friend,

When I contemplate the nations of the earth, and their conduct towards each other, through the medium of a scriptural light, my opinions of them are exactly like your own. Whether they do good or do evil, I see them acting under the permission or direction of that Providence who governs the earth, whose operations are as irresistible as they are silent and unsuspected. So far we are perfectly agreed; and howsoever we may differ upon inferior parts of the subject, it is, as you say, an affair of no great consequence. For instance, you think the peace a better than we deserve, and in a certain sense I agree with you: as a sinful nation we deserve no peace at all, and have reason enough to be thankful that the voice of war is at any rate put to silence.

[...]

Mrs Unwin thanks Mrs Newton for her kind letter, and for executing her commissions. We truly love you both, and think of you often.

W.C.

XLV *To William Unwin*   4 August 1783

My Dear William,

I feel myself sensibly obliged by the interest you take in the success of my productions. Your feelings upon the subject are such as I should have myself, had I an opportunity of calling Johnson aside to make the enquiry you purpose. But I am pretty well prepared for the worst, and so long as I have the opinion of a few capable judges in my favour, and am thereby convinced that I have neither disgraced myself nor my subject, shall not feel myself disposed to any extreme anxiety about the sale. To aim with success at the spiritual good of mankind, and to become popular by writing on scriptural subjects, were an unreasonable ambition, even for a poet to entertain, in days like these. Verse may have many charms, but has none powerful enough to conquer the aversion of a dissipated age to such instruction. Ask the question therefore boldly, and be not mortified even though he should shake his head, and drop his chin, for it is no more than we have reason to expect. We will lay the fault upon the vice of the times, and we will acquit the poet.

[...] I have two goldfinches, which in the summer occupy the greenhouse. A few days since, being employed in cleaning out their cages, I placed that which I had in hand upon the table, while the other hung against the wall: the windows and the doors stood wide open. I went to fill the fountain at the pump, and on my return was not a little surprised to find a goldfinch sitting on the top of the cage I had been cleaning, and singing to and kissing the goldfinch within. I approached him, and he discovered no fear; still nearer, and he discovered none. I advanced my hand towards him, and he took no notice of it. I seized him, and supposed I had caught a new bird, but casting my eye upon the other cage perceived my mistake. Its inhabitant, during my absence, had contrived to find an opening, where the wire had been a little bent, and made no other use of the escape it afforded him, than to salute his friend, and to converse with him more intimately than he had done before. I returned him to his proper mansion, but in vain. In less than a minute he had thrust his little person through the aperture again, and again perched upon his neighbour's cage, kissing him, as at the first, and singing, as if transported with the fortunate adventure. I could not but respect such friendship, as for the sake of its gratification had twice declined an opportunity to be free, and, consenting to their union, resolved that for the future one cage should hold them both. I am glad of such incidents; for at a pinch, and when I need entertainment, the versification of them serves to divert me.

[...] – Yours ever,

W.C.

XLVI *To William Unwin*   29 September 1783

My Dear William,

We are sorry that you and your household partake so largely of the ill effects of this unhealthy season. You are happy however in having hitherto escaped the epidemic fever, which has prevailed much in this part of the kingdom, and carried many off. Your mother and I are well. After more than a fortnight's indisposition, which slight appellation is quite adequate to the description of all I suffered, I am at length restored by a grain or two of emetic tartar. It is a tax I generally pay in autumn. By this time, I hope, a purer ether than we have seen for months, and these brighter suns than the summer had to boast, have cheered your spirits, and made your existence more comfortable. We are rational; but we are animal too, and therefore subject to the influences of the weather. The cattle in the fields show evident symptoms of lassitude and disgust in an unpleasant season; and we, their lords and masters, are constrained to sympathize with them: the only difference between us is, that they know not the cause of their dejection, and we do, – but, for our humiliation, are equally at a loss to cure it. Upon this account I have sometimes wished myself a philosopher. How happy, in comparison with myself, does the sagacious investigator of nature seem, whose fancy is ever employed in the invention of *hypotheses*, and his reason in the support of them! While he is accounting for the origin of the winds, he has no leisure to attend to their influence upon himself; and while he considers what the sun is made of, forgets that he has not shone for a month. One project indeed supplants another. The *vortices* of Descartes gave way to the gravitation of Newton, and this again is threatened by the electrical fluid of a modern. One generation blows bubbles, and the next breaks them. But in the mean time your philosopher is a happy man. He escapes a thousand inquietudes to which the indolent are subject, and finds his occupation, whether it be the pursuit of a butterfly, or a demonstration, the wholesomest exercise in the world. As he proceeds, he applauds himself. His discoveries, though eventually perhaps they prove but dreams, are to him realities. The world gaze at him, as he does at new phenomena in the heavens, and perhaps understand him as little. But this does not prevent their praises, nor at all disturb him in the enjoyment of that self-complacence, to which his imaginary success entitles him. He wears his honours while he lives, and if another strips them off when he has been dead a century, it is no great matter; he can then make shift without them.

I have said a great deal upon this subject, and know not what it all amounts to. I did not intend a syllable of it when I began.

But *currente calamo*, I stumbled upon it. My end is to amuse myself and you. The former of these two points is secured. I shall be happy if I do not miss the latter.

By the way, what is your opinion of these air-balloons? I am quite charmed with the discovery. Is it not possible (do you suppose) to convey such a quantity of inflammable air into the stomach and abdomen, that the philosopher, no longer gravitating to a centre, shall ascend by his own comparative levity, and never stop till he has reached the medium exactly *in equilibrio* with himself? May he not by the help of a pasteboard rudder, attached to his posteriors, steer himself in that purer element with ease; and again by a slow and gradual discharge of his aerial contents, recover his former tendency to the earth, and descend without the smallest danger or inconvenience? These things are worth inquiry; and (I dare say) they will be inquired after as they deserve. The *pennae non homini datae*, are likely to be less regretted than they were; and perhaps a flight of academicians and a covey of fine ladies may be no uncommon spectacle in the next generation. A letter which appeared in the public prints last week convinces me, that the learned are not without hopes of some such improvement upon this discovery. The author is a sensible and ingenious man, and under a reasonable apprehension that the ignorant may feel themselves inclined to laugh upon a subject that affects himself with the utmost seriousness, with much good manners and management bespeaks their patience, suggesting many good consequences that may result from a course of experiments upon this machine, and amongst others, that it may be of use in ascertaining the shape of continents and islands, and the face of wide-extended and far distant countries; an end not to be hoped for, unless by these means of extraordinary elevation the human prospect may be immensely enlarged, and the philosopher, exalted to the skies, attain a view of the whole hemisphere at once. But whether he is to ascend by the mere inflation of his person, as hinted above, or whether in a sort of bandbox, supported upon balloons, is not yet apparent, nor (I suppose) even in his own idea perfectly decided. – Yours, my dear William,

W.C.

My Dear William,

[...]

Last Saturday se'nnight, the moment I had composed myself in my bed, your mother too having just got into hers, we were alarmed by a cry of fire on the staircase. I immediately rose, and saw sheets of flame above the roof of Mr Palmer's house, our opposite neighbour. The mischief however was not so near to him as it seemed to be, having begun in a butcher's yard, at a little distance. We made all haste down stairs, and soon threw open the street door, for the reception of as much lumber, of all sorts, as our house would hold, brought into it by several who thought it necessary to move their furniture. In two hours time we had so much that we could hold no more, even the uninhabited part of our building being filled. Not that we ourselves were entirely secure – an adjoining thatch, on which fell showers of sparks, being rather a dangerous neighbour. Providentially, however, the night was perfectly calm, and we escaped. By four in the morning it was extinguished, having consumed many out-buildings, but no dwelling-house. Your mother suffered a little in her health, from the fatigue and bustle of the night, but soon recovered. As for me, it hurt me not. The slightest wind would have carried the fire to the very extremity of the town, there being multitudes of thatched buildings and faggot-piles so near to each other, that they must have proved infallible conductors.

The balloons prosper; and I congratulate you upon it. Thanks to Montgolfier, we shall fly at last. – Yours, my dear friend,

W.C.

My Dear Friend,

A parcel arrived last night, the contents of which shall be disposed of according to order. We thank Mrs Newton (not from the teeth outwards) for the tooth-brushes.

The country around us is much alarmed with apprehensions of fire. Two have happened since that of Olney. One at Hitchin, where the damage is said to amount to eleven thousand pounds, and another, at a place not far from Hitchin, of which I have not learnt the name. Letters have been dropped at Bedford, threatening to burn the town; and the inhabitants have been so intimidated as to have placed a guard in many parts of it, several nights past. Some madman or some devil has broke loose, who it is to be hoped will pay dear for these effusions of his malignity. Since our conflagration here, we have sent two women and a boy to the justice, for depredation; Sue Riviss, for stealing a piece of beef, which, in her excuse, she said she intended to take care of. This lady, whom you well remember, escaped for want of evidence; not that evidence was indeed wanting, but our men of Gotham judged it unnecessary to send it. With her went the woman I mentioned before, who, it seems, has made some sort of profession, but upon this occasion allowed herself a latitude of conduct rather inconsistent with it, having filled her apron with wearing apparel, which she likewise intended to take care of. She would have gone to the county gaol, had Billy Raban, the baker's son, who prosecuted, insisted upon it; but he good-naturedly, though I think weakly, interposed in her favour, and begged her off. The young gentleman who accompanied these fair ones, is the junior son of Molly Boswell. He had stolen some iron-work, the property of Griggs, the butcher. Being convicted, he was ordered to be whipt, which operation he underwent at the cart's tail, from the stone-house to the high arch, and back again. He seemed to show great fortitude, but it was all an imposition upon the public. The beadle, who performed it, had filled his left hand with red ochre, through which, after every stroke, he drew the lash of his whip, leaving the appearance of a wound upon the skin, but in reality not hurting him at all. This being perceived by Mr Constable Hinschcomb, who followed the beadle, he applied his cane, without any such management or precaution, to the shoulders of the too merciful executioner. The scene immediately became more interesting. The beadle could by no means be prevailed upon to strike hard, which provoked the constable to strike harder; and this double flogging continued, till a lass of Silver-end, pitying the pitiful beadle thus suffering under the hands of the pitiless constable, joined the procession, and placing herself immediately behind the latter, seized him by his capillary club, and pulling him backwards by the same, slapt his face with a most Amazonian fury. This concatenation of events has taken up more of my paper than I intended it should, but I could not forbear to inform you how the beadle threshed the thief, the constable the beadle, and the lady the constable, and how the thief was the only person concerned who suffered nothing.

[...]

I beg you will accept for yourself and yours our unfeigned love, and remember me affectionately to Mr Bacon, when you see him. – Yours, my dear friend,

Wm. Cowper

XLIX *To William Bull*   22 February 1784

William Bull, the dissenting clergyman of Newport Pagnall, was introduced to Cowper by Newton and became a close friend of the poet. The 'Sofa' to which this letter refers was to become the opening book of *The Task*. At this stage of the composition, though, 'Sofa' appears to be the projected title of the entire poem.

I congratulate you on the thaw – I suppose it is an universal blessing, and probably felt all over Europe. I myself am the better for it, who wanted nothing that might make the frost supportable; what reason, therefore, have they to rejoice, who, being in want of all things, were exposed to its utmost rigour? The ice in my ink, however, is not yet dissolved. It was long before the frost seized it, but at last it prevailed. The Sofa has consequently received little or no addition since. It consists at present of four books, and part of a fifth; when the sixth is finished, the work is accomplished, but if I may judge by my present inability, that period is at a considerable distance.

L *To John Newton*   19 March 1784

The 'Collins' mentioned here is William Collins (1721–1759), a writer of odes who, like Cowper, was subject to bouts of madness and depression. Although a relatively unsuccessful writer during his lifetime, he became popular and influential later in the century, particularly with the Romantic poets.

My Dear Friend,
    [...]
My evenings are devoted to books. I read aloud for the entertainment of the party, thus making amends by a vociferation of two hours for my silence at other times.

I have lately finished eight volumes of Johnson's *Prefaces*, or *Lives of the Poets*. In all that number I observe but one man, – a poet of no great fame, – of whom I did not know that he existed till I found him there, whose mind seems to have had the slightest tincture of religion; and he was hardly in his senses. His name was Collins. He sunk into a state of melancholy, and died young. Not long before his death, he was found at his lodgings in Islington by his biographer, with the New Testament in his hand. He said to Johnson, 'I have but one book, but it is the best.' Of him, therefore, there are some hopes. But from the lives of all the rest there is but one inference to be drawn: – that poets are a very worthless, wicked set of people.

Mrs Unwin sends her love; she is much obliged to Mrs Newton for the care she has taken about the worsted. She had no suspicion that Mrs Newton had forgot it, but supposed her correspondent might. We are in good health, and waiting as patiently as we can for the end of this second winter. The news is – that the brother of farmer Rush, a very sober young man, was driving his waggon last week to Bedford, and in the way ordered his man forward with the team, saying he would follow him, but he has never been heard of since. – Yours, my dear friends, truly,

Wm. C.

My Dear Friend,
[...]
Balloons are so much the mode, that even in this country we have attempted a balloon. You may possibly remember that at a place called Weston, little more than a mile from Olney, there lives a family whose name is Throckmorton. The present possessor of the estate is a young man whom I remember a boy. He has a wife, who is young, genteel, and handsome. They are Papists, but much more amiable than many Protestants. We never had any intercourse with the family, though ever since we lived here we have enjoyed the range of their pleasure grounds, having been favoured with a key, which admits us into all. When this man succeeded to the estate, on the death of his elder brother, and came to settle at Weston, I sent him a complimentary card, requesting the continuance of that privilege, having till then enjoyed it by the favour of his mother, who on that occasion went to finish her days at Bath. You may conclude that he granted it, and for about two years nothing more passed between us. A fortnight ago, I received an invitation in the civilest terms, in which he told me that the next day he should attempt to fill a balloon, and if it would be any pleasure to me to be present, should be happy to see me. Your mother and I went. The whole country were there, but the balloon could not be filled. The endeavour was, I believe, very philosophically made, but such a process depends for its success upon such niceties as make it very precarious. Our reception was however flattering to a great degree, insomuch that more notice seemed to be taken of us, than we could possibly have expected; indeed rather more than of any of his

71

other guests. They even seemed anxious to recommend themselves to our regards. We drank chocolate, and were asked to dine, but were engaged. A day or two afterwards, Mrs Unwin and I walked that way, and were overtaken in a shower. I found a tree that I thought would shelter us both, – a large elm, in a grove that fronts the mansion. Mrs T. observed us, and running towards us in the rain insisted on our walking in. He was gone out. We sat chatting with her till the weather cleared up, and then at her instance took a walk with her in the garden. The garden is almost their only walk, and is certainly their only retreat in which they are not liable to interruption. She offered us a key of it in a manner that made it impossible not to accept it, and said she would send us one. A few days afterwards, in the cool of the evening, we walked that way again. We saw them going toward the house, and exchanged bows and curtsies at a little distance, but did not join them. In a few minutes, when we had passed the house, and had almost reached the gate that opens out of the park into the adjoining field, I heard the iron gate belonging to the court-yard ring, and saw Mr T. advancing hastily toward us; we made equal haste to meet him, he presented to us the key, which I told him I esteemed a singular favour, and after a few such speeches as are made on such occasions, we parted. This happened about a week ago. I concluded nothing less, than that all this civility and attention was designed, on their part, as a prelude to a nearer acquaintance; but here at present the matter rests. I should like exceedingly to be on an easy footing there, to give a morning call, and now and then to receive one, but nothing more. For though he is one of the most agreeable men I ever saw, I could not wish to visit him in any other way, neither our house, furniture, servants, or income, being such as qualify us to make entertainments; neither would I on any account be introduced to the neighbouring gentry, which must be the consequence of our dining there, there not being a man in the country, except himself, with whom I could endure to associate. They are squires, merely such, purse-proud and sportsmen. But Mr T. is altogether a man of fashion, and respectable on every account.

I have told you a long story. Farewell. We number the days

as they pass, and are glad that we shall see you and your sister soon. – Yours, &c.

W.C.

LII *To John Newton*   22 May 1784

My Dear Friend,

I am glad to have received at last an account of Dr Johnson's favourable opinion of my book. I thought it wanting, and had long since concluded, that, not having had the happiness to please him, I owed my ignorance of his sentiments to the tenderness of my friends at Hoxton, who would not mortify me with an account of his disapprobation. It occurs to me that I owe him thanks for interposing between me and the resentment of the Reviewers, who seldom show mercy to an advocate for evangelical truth, whether in prose or verse. I therefore enclose a short acknowledgment, which, if you see no impropriety in the measure, you can, I imagine, without much difficulty convey to him through the hands of Mr Latrobe. If on any account you judge it an inexpedient step, you can very easily suppress the letter.

[…] – Yours, my dear friend,

W.C.

LIII *To the* Gentleman's Magazine   28 May 1784

This letter was printed as an article on 28 May 1784. It takes up the subject of hares that Cowper discussed in letter XXIII.

In the year 1774, being much indisposed both in mind and body, incapable of diverting myself either with company or books, and yet in a condition that made some diversion necessary, I was glad of anything that would engage my attention without fatiguing it. The children of a neighbour of mine had a leveret given them for a plaything; it was at that time about three months old. Understanding better how to tease the poor creature than to feed it, and soon becoming weary of their charge, they readily consented that their father, who saw it pining and growing leaner every day, should offer it to my acceptance. I was willing enough to take the prisoner under my protection, perceiving that, in the management of such an animal, and in the attempt to tame it, I should find just that sort of employment which my case required. It was soon known among the neighbours that I was pleased with the present, and the consequence was, that in a short time I had as many leverets offered to me as would have stocked a paddock. I undertook the care of three, which it is necessary that I should here distinguish by the names I gave them – Puss, Tiney, and Bess. Notwithstanding the two feminine appellatives, I must inform you that they were all males. Immediately commencing carpenter, I built them houses to sleep in; each had a separate apartment, so contrived that their ordure would pass through the bottom of it; an earthen pan placed under each received whatsoever fell, which being duly emptied and washed, they were thus kept perfectly sweet and clean. In the daytime they had the range of a hall, and at night retired each to his own bed, never intruding into that of another.

Puss grew presently familiar, would leap into my lap, raise himself upon his hinder feet, and bite the hair from my temples. He would suffer me to take him up, and to carry him about in my arms, and has more than once fallen fast asleep upon my knee. He was ill three days, during which time I nursed him, kept him apart from his fellows, that they might not molest him (for, like many other wild animals, they persecute one of their own species that is sick), and by constant care, and trying him with a variety of herbs, restored him to perfect health. No creature could be more grateful than my patient after his recovery; a sentiment which he most significantly expressed by licking my hand, first the back of it, then the palm, then every finger separately, then between all the fingers, as if anxious to leave no part of it unsaluted; a ceremony which he never performed but once again upon a similar occasion. Finding him extremely tractable, I made it my custom to carry him always after breakfast into the garden, where he hid himself generally under the leaves of a cucumber vine, sleeping, or chewing the cud till evening; in the leaves also of that vine he found a favourite repast. I had not long habituated him to this taste of liberty, before he began to be impatient for the return of the time when he might enjoy it. He would invite me to the garden by drumming upon my knee, and by a look of such expression as it was not possible to misinterpret. If this rhetoric did not immediately succeed, he would take the skirt of my coat between his teeth, and pull it with all his force. Thus Puss might be said to be perfectly tamed, the shyness of his nature was done away, and on the whole it was visible, by many symptoms which I have not room to enumerate, that he was happier in human society than when shut up with his natural companions.

Not so Tiney; upon him the kindest treatment had not the least effect. He too was sick, and in his sickness had an equal share of my attention; but if, after his recovery, I took the liberty to stroke him, he would grunt, strike with his fore-feet, spring forward, and bite. He was, however, very entertaining in his way; even his surliness was matter of mirth, and in his play he preserved such an air of gravity, and performed his feats with such a solemnity of manner, that in him too I had an agreeable companion.

Bess, who died soon after he was full grown, and whose death was occasioned by his being turned into his box, which had been washed, while it was yet damp, was a hare of great humour and drollery. Puss was tamed by gentle usage; Tiney was not to be tamed at all; and Bess had a courage and confidence that made him tame from the beginning. I always admitted them into the parlour after supper, when, the carpet affording their feet a firm hold, they would frisk, and bound, and play a thousand gambols, in which Bess, being remarkably strong and fearless, was always superior to the rest, and proved himself the Vestris of the party. One evening the cat, being in the room, had the hardiness to pat Bess upon the cheek, an indignity which he resented by drumming upon her back with such violence, that the cat was happy to escape from under his paws, and hide herself.

I describe these animals as having each a character of his own. Such they were, in fact, and their countenances were so expressive of that character, that, when I looked only on the face of either, I immediately knew which it was. It is said that a shepherd, however numerous his flock, soon becomes so familiar with their features, that he can, by that indication only, distinguish each from all the rest; and yet, to a common observer, the difference is hardly perceptible. I doubt not that the same discrimination in the cast of countenances would be discoverable in hares, and am persuaded that among a thousand of them no two could be found exactly similar, a circumstance little suspected by those who have not had opportunity to observe it. These creatures have a singular sagacity in discovering the minutest alteration that is made in the place to which they are accustomed, and instantly apply their nose to the examination of a new object. A small hole being burnt in the carpet, it was mended with a patch, and that patch in a moment underwent the strictest scrutiny. They seem, too, to be very much directed by the smell in the choice of their favourites; to some persons, though they saw them daily, they could never be reconciled, and would even scream when they attempted to touch them; but a miller coming in, engaged their affections at once; his powdered coat had charms that were irresistible. It is no wonder that my intimate acquaintance with these specimens of the kind, has taught me to hold the sportsman's amusement in abhorrence. He little knows what amiable creatures he persecutes, of what gratitude they are capable, how cheerful they are in their spirits, what enjoyment they have of life, and that, impressed as they seem with a peculiar dread of man, it is only because man gives them peculiar cause for it.

[...]

Bess, I have said, died young. Tiney lived to be nine years old, and died at last, I have reason to think, of some hurt in his loins by a fall. Puss is still living, and has just completed his tenth year, discovering no signs of decay, nor even of age, except that he is grown more discreet and less frolicsome than he was. I cannot conclude without observing, that I have lately introduced a dog to his acquaintance – a spaniel that had never seen a hare, to a hare that had never seen a spaniel. I did it with great caution, but there was no real need of it. Puss discovered no token of fear, nor Marquis the least symptom of hostility. There is, therefore, it should seem, no natural antipathy between dog and hare; but the pursuit of the one occasions the flight of the other, and the dog pursues because he is trained to it. They eat bread at the same time out of the same hand, and are in all respects sociable and friendly.

I should not do complete justice to my subject, did I not add, that they have no ill scent belonging to them, that they are indefatigably nice in keeping themselves clean, for which purpose nature has furnished them with a brush under each foot; and that they are never infested by any vermin.

LIV *To John Newton*   5 June 1784

As far as it is possible to ascertain, it does not seem probable that Samuel Johnson read Cowper's *Poems*.

When you told me that the critique upon my volume was written, though not by Dr Johnson himself, yet by a friend of his, to whom he recommended the book and the business, I inferred from that expression that I was indebted to him for an active interposition in my favour, and consequently that he had a right to thanks. But now I concur entirely in sentiment with you, and heartily second your vote for the suppression of thanks which do not seem to be much called for. Yet even now, were it possible that I could fall into his company, I should not think a slight acknowledgment misapplied. I was no other way anxious about his opinion, nor could be so, after you and some others had given a favourable one, than it was natural I should be, knowing, as I did, that his opinion had been consulted. – I am affectionately yours,

                                                                          W.C.

From the moment he completed the *Poems*, Cowper had been contemplating another volume of verse. In October 1783, he began work on *The Task*, which would eventually make up practically all of this volume, the other poems being 'An Epistle to Joseph Hill, Esq.', 'Tirocinium: or, A Review of Schools' and 'The Diverting History of John Gilpin'. Apart from an earlier letter to Bull (see letter XLIX), Cowper rarely mentions the progress of the poem during the period of its composition. However, this letter and the following ones to Unwin, Newton, Hill and Joseph Johnson are some of Cowper's most significant summaries of the style and content of his major poem.

My Dear Friend,

I received your letter on the first. I answer on the third. You leave Lymington on the sixth, and will consequently be at home when you receive my answer. I shall not therefore be very prolix, writing as I do, under the expectation and hope that we shall see you soon.

We are both indebted and obliged to you for your journal of occurrences, and are glad that there is not one amongst them for which *you* have reason to be sorry. Your seaside situation, your beautiful prospects, your fine rides, and the sight of the palaces which you have seen, we have not envied you; but are glad that you have enjoyed them. Why should we envy any man? Is not our greenhouse a cabinet of perfumes? It is at this moment fronted with carnations and balsalms, with mignionette and roses, with jessamine and woodbine, and wants nothing but your pipe to make it truly Arabian; – a wilderness of sweets! The *Sofa* is ended, but not finished; a paradox, which your natural acumen, sharpened by habits of logical attention, will enable you to reconcile in a moment. Do not imagine, however, that I lounge over it; on the contrary I find it severe exercise, to mould and fashion it to my mind!

Let us see you as soon as possible; present our affectionate respects to your family, and tell the Welshman and his chum that if they do not behave themselves well, I will lash them soundly; they will not be the first academics to whom I have shown no mercy. – Yours, with Mrs Unwin's love,

Wm. Cowper

LVI *To William Unwin*   10 October 1784

My Dear William,

I send you four quires of verse, which having sent, I shall dismiss from my thoughts, and think no more of, till I see them in print. I have not after all found time or industry enough to give the last hand to the points. I believe, however, they are not very erroneous, though in so long a work, and in a work that requires nicety in this particular, some inaccuracies will escape. Where you find any, you will oblige me by correcting them.

In some passages, especially in the second book, you will observe me very satirical. Writing on such subjects I could not be otherwise. I can write nothing without aiming at least at usefulness: it were beneath my years to do it, and still more dishonourable to my religion. I know that a reformation of such abuses as I have censured is not to be expected from the efforts of a poet; but to contemplate the world, its follies, its vices, its indifference to duty, and its strenuous attachment to what is evil, and not to reprehend, were to approve it. From this charge at least I shall be clear, for I have neither tacitly nor expressly flattered either its characters or its customs. [...]

What there is of a religious cast in the volume I have thrown towards the end of it, for two reasons; first, that I might not revolt the reader at his entrance, – and secondly, that my best impressions might be made last. Were I to write as many volumes as Lope de Vega, or Voltaire, not one of them would be without this tincture. If the world like it not, so much the worse for them. I make all the concessions I can, that I may please them, but I will not please them at the expense of conscience.

My descriptions are all from nature: not one of them second-handed. My delineations of the heart are from my own experience: not one of them borrowed from books, or in the least degree conjectural. In my numbers, which I have varied as much as I could, (for blank verse without variety of numbers is no better than bladder and string,) I have imitated nobody, though sometimes perhaps there may be an apparent resemblance; because at the same time that I would not imitate, I have not affectedly differed.

If the work cannot boast a regular plan, (in which respect however I do not think it altogether indefensible,) it may yet boast, that the reflections are naturally suggested always by the preceding passage, and that except the fifth book, which is rather of a political aspect, the whole has one tendency; to discountenance the modern enthusiasm after a London life, and to recommend rural ease and leisure, as friendly to the cause of piety and virtue.

If it pleases you I shall be happy, and collect from your pleasure in it an omen of its general acceptance. – Yours, my dear friend,

W.C.

LVII *To John Newton*   30 October 1784

My Dear Friend,
  [...]
I am again at Johnson's in the shape of a poem in blank verse, consisting of six books, and called *The Task*. I began it about this time twelvemonth, and writing sometimes an hour in a day, sometimes half a one, and sometimes two hours, have lately finished it. I mentioned it not sooner, because almost to the last I was doubtful whether I should ever bring it to a conclusion, working often in such distress of mind, as, while it spurred me to the work, at the same time threatened to disqualify me for it. My bookseller I suppose will be as tardy as before. I do not expect to be born into the world till the month of March, when I and the crocuses shall peep together. You may assure yourself

that I shall take my first opportunity to wait on you. I mean like-wise to gratify myself by obtruding my Muse upon Mr Bacon.

Adieu, my dear friend! we are well, and love you. – Yours, and Mrs Newton's,

W.C.

LVIII *To Joseph Hill*   November 1784

My Dear Friend,

To condole with you on the death of a mother aged eighty-seven would be absurd; rather, therefore, as is reasonable, I congratulate you on the almost singular felicity of having enjoyed the company of so amiable, and so near a relation so long. Your lot and mine in this respect have been very different, as indeed in almost every other. Your mother lived to see you rise, at least to see you comfortably established in the world: mine, dying when I was six years old, did not live to see me sink in it. You may remember with pleasure, while you live, a blessing vouchsafed to you so long; and I, while I live, must regret a comfort of which I was deprived so early. I can truly say, that not a week passes, (perhaps I might with equal veracity say a day,) in which I do not think of her. Such was the impression her tenderness made upon me, though the opportunity she had for showing it was so short. But the ways of God are equal; – and when I reflect on the pangs she would have suffered, had she been a witness of all mine, I see more cause to rejoice than to mourn, that she was hidden in the grave so soon.

[...]

I am gone to the press again; a volume of mine will greet your hands some time either in the course of the winter, or early in the spring. You will find it perhaps on the whole more entertaining than the former, as it treats a greater variety of subjects, and those, at least the most, of a sublunary kind. It will consist of a poem, in six books, called *The Task*. To which will be added another, which I finished yesterday, called, I believe, *Tirocinium*, on the subject of education.

81

You perceive that I have taken your advice, and given the pen no rest.

W.C.

LIX *To John Newton*   11 December 1784

My Dear Friend,

Having imitated no man, I may reasonably hope that I shall not incur the disadvantage of a comparison with my betters. Milton's manner was peculiar. So is Thomson's. He that should write like either of them, would, in my judgement, deserve the name of a copyist, but not of a poet. A judicious and sensible reader, therefore, like yourself will not say that my manner is not good, because it does not resemble theirs, but will rather consider what it is in itself. Blank verse is susceptible of a much greater diversification of manner, than verse in rhyme: and why the modern writers of it have all thought proper to cast their numbers alike, I know not. Certainly it was not necessity that compelled them to it. I flatter myself however that I have avoided that sameness with others, which would entitle me to nothing but a share in one common oblivion with them all. It is possible that, as the reviewer of my former volume found cause to say that he knew not to what class of writers to refer me, the reviewer of this, whosoever he shall be, may see occasion to remark the same singularity. At any rate, though as little apt to be sanguine as most men, and more prone to fear and despond, than to overrate my own productions, I am persuaded that I shall not forfeit any thing by this volume that I gained by the last.

As to the title, I take it to be the best that is to be had. It is not possible that a book, including such a variety of subjects, and in which no particular one is predominant, should find a title adapted to them all. In such a case, it seemed almost necessary to accommodate the name to the incident that gave birth to the poem; nor does it appear to me, that because I performed more than my task, therefore *The Task* is not a suitable title. A house would still be a house, though the builder of it should make it ten times as big as he at first intended. I might indeed, following the example of the Sunday newsmonger, call it *The Olio*. But I should do myself wrong; for though it have much variety, it has, I trust, no confusion.

For the same reason none of the interior titles apply themselves to the contents at large of that book to which they belong. They are, every one of them, taken either from the leading, (I should say the introductory,) passage of that particular book, or from that which makes the most conspicuous figure in it. Had I set off with a design to write upon a gridiron, and had I actually written near two hundred lines upon that utensil, as I have upon the Sofa, *The Gridiron* should have been my title. But the Sofa being, as I may say, the starting-post from which I addressed myself to the long race that I soon conceived a design to run, it acquired a just pre-eminence in my account, and was very worthily advanced to the titular honour it enjoys, its right being at least so far a good one, that no word in the language could pretend a better.

The Time-piece appears to me, (though by some accident the import of that title has escaped you,) to have a degree of propriety beyond the most of them. The book to which it belongs is intended to strike the hour that gives notice of approaching judgement, and dealing pretty largely in the signs of the times, seems to be denominated, as it is, with a sufficient degree of accommodation to the subject.

[...]

We are truly sorry for Mrs Newton's indisposition, and shall be glad to hear of her recovery. We are most liable to colds at this season, and at this season a cold is most difficult of cure.

Be pleased to remember us to the young ladies, and to all under your roof and elsewhere, who are mindful of us. – And believe me, your affectionate,

Wm. Cowper

[...]

I did not write the line, that has been tampered with, hastily, or without due attention to the construction of it; and what appeared to me its only merit is, in its present state, entirely annihilated.

I know that the ears of modern verse-writers are delicate to an excess, and their readers are troubled with the same squeamishness as themselves. So that if a line do not run as smooth as quicksilver they are offended. A critic of the present day serves a poem as a cook serves a dead turkey, when she fastens the legs of it to a post, and draws out all the sinews. For this we may thank Pope; but unless we could imitate him in the closeness and compactness of his expression, as well as in the smoothness of his numbers, we had better drop the imitation, which serves no other purpose than to emasculate and weaken all we write. Give me a manly, rough line, with a deal of meaning in it, rather than a whole poem full of musical periods, that have nothing but their oily smoothness to recommend them!

I have said thus much, as I hinted in the beginning, because I have just finished a much longer poem than the last, which our common friend will receive by the same messenger that has the charge of this letter. In that poem there are many lines, which an ear, so nice as the gentleman's who made the above mentioned alteration, would undoubtedly condemn; and yet (if I may be permitted to say it) they cannot be made smoother without being the worse for it. There is a roughness on a plum, which nobody that understands fruit would rub off, though the plum would be much more polished without it. But lest I tire you, I will only add, that I wish you to guard me from all such meddling; assuring you, that I always write as smoothly as I can; but that I never did, never will, sacrifice the spirit or sense of a passage to the sound of it.

Samuel Johnson died on 13 December 1784, and was buried on 20 December in Westminster Abbey.

Jean-Pierre Bluchard crossed the channel from England to France on 7 January 1784. This was the first channel crossing by hot air balloon.

My Dear William,

Your letters are always welcome. You can always either find something to say, or can amuse me and yourself with a sociable and friendly way of saying nothing. I never found that a letter was the more easily written, because the writing of it had been long delayed. On the contrary, experience has taught me to answer soon, that I may do it without difficulty. It is in vain to wait for an accumulation of materials in a situation such as yours and mine, productive of few events. At the end of our expectations we shall find ourselves as poor as at the beginning.

I can hardly tell you with any certainty of information, upon what terms Mr Newton and I may be supposed to stand at present. A month, I believe, has passed, since I heard from him. But my *friseur*, having been in London in the course of this week, whence he returned last night, and having called at Hoxton, brought me his love, and an excuse for his silence, which (he said) had been occasioned by the frequency of his preachings at this season. He was not pleased that my manuscript was not first transmitted to him, and I have cause to suspect that he was even mortified at being informed, that a certain inscribed poem was not inscribed to himself. But we shall jumble together again, as people that have an affection for each other at bottom, notwithstanding now and then a slight disagreement, always do.

[...]

The death of Dr Johnson has set a thousand scribblers to work, and me among the rest. While I lay in bed, waiting till I could reasonably hope that the parlour might be ready for me, I invoked the muse, and composed the following

Epitaph

Here Johnson lies, a sage by all allow'd,
Whom to have bred may well make England proud;
Whose prose was eloquence, by wisdom taught,
The graceful vehicle of virtuous thought;
Whose verse may claim, grave, masculine, and strong,
Superior praise to the mere poet's song;
Who many a noble gift from Heaven possess'd,
And faith at last, alone worth all the rest:
O man, immortal by a double prize, –
By fame on earth, by glory in the skies!

[...]

You and your family have our sincere love. Forget not to present my respectful compliments to Miss Unwin, and, if you have not done it already, thank her on my part for the very agreeable narrative of Lunardi. He is a young man, I presume, of great good sense and spirit, (his letters at least, and his enterprising turn, bespeak him such,) a man qualified to shine not only among the stars, but in the more useful, though humbler sphere of terrestrial occupation.

I have been crossing the Channel in a balloon, ever since I read of that achievement by Blanchard. I have an insatiable thirst to know the philosophical reason, why his vehicle had like to have fallen into the sea, when for aught that appears the gas was not at all exhausted. Did not the extreme cold condense the inflammable air, and cause the globe to collapse? Tell me, and be my Apollo for ever! – Affectionately yours,

W.C.

LXII *To William Unwin*   20 March 1785

In March 1785, Cowper was preparing the proofs of *The Task* as signs of a conflict between Joseph II, the Holy Roman Emperor, and the Dutch who were refusing his claim to their country, became more ominous.

My Dear William,

I thank you for your letter. It made me laugh, and there are not many things capable of being contained within the dimensions of a letter, for which I see cause to be more thankful. I was pleased too to see my opinion of his Lordship's *nonchalance* upon a subject that you had so much at heart, completely verified. I do not know that the eye of a nobleman was ever dissected. I cannot help supposing however that, were that organ, as it exists in the head of such a personage, to be accurately examined, it would be found to differ materially in its construction from the eye of a commoner; so very different is the view that men in an elevated, and in an humble station, have of the same object. What appears great, sublime, beautiful, and important, to you and to me, when submitted to the notice of my lord, or his grace, and submitted too with the utmost humility, is either too minute to be visible at all, or if seen, seems trivial, and of no account. My supposition therefore seems not altogether chimerical.

In two months I have corrected proof sheets to the amount of ninety-six pages, and no more. In other words, I have received three packets. Nothing is quick enough for impatience, and I suppose that the impatience of an author has the quickest of all possible movements. It appears to me however that at this rate we shall not publish till next autumn. Should you happen therefore to pass Johnson's door, pop in your head as you go, and just insinuate to him, that, were his remittances rather more frequent, that frequency would be no inconvenience to me. I much expected one this evening, a fortnight having now elapsed since the arrival of the last. But none came, and I felt myself a little mortified. I took up the newspaper however, and read it. There I found that the emperor and the Dutch are, after all their negotiations, going to war. Such reflections as these struck me. A great part of Europe is going to be involved in the greatest of all calamities; – troops are in motion, – artillery is drawn together, – cabinets are busied in contriving schemes of blood and devastation, – thousands will perish, who are incapable of understanding the dispute; and thousands, who, whatever the event may be, are little more interested in it than myself, will suffer unspeakable hardships in the course of the quarrel: – Well! Mr Poet, and how then? You have composed certain verses, which you are desirous to see in print, and because the impression seems to be delayed, you are displeased, not to say dispirited; – be ashamed of yourself! you live in a world in which your feelings may find worthier subjects, – be concerned for the havoc of nations, and mourn over your retarded volume when you find a dearth of more important tragedies!

[...] – Adieu,

W.C.

LXIII *To William Unwin*   30 April 1785

My Dear Friend,

I return you thanks for a letter so warm with the intelligence of the celebrity of *John Gilpin*. I little thought, when I mounted him upon my Pegasus, that he would become so famous. I have learned also, from Mr Newton, that he is equally renowned in Scotland, and that a lady there had undertaken to write a second part, on the subject of Mrs Gilpin's return to London, but not succeeding in it as she wished, she dropped it. He tells me likewise, that the head master of St. Paul's school, (who he is I know not,) has conceived, in consequence of the entertainment that John has afforded him, a vehement desire to write to me. Let us hope he will alter his mind; for should we even exchange civilities upon the occasion, *Tirocinium* will spoil all. The great estimation however in which this knight of the stone-bottles is held, may turn out a circumstance propitious to the volume of which his history will make a part. Those events that prove the prelude to our greatest success, are often apparently trivial in themselves, and such as seemed to promise nothing. The disappointment that Horace mentions is reversed – We design a mug, and it proves a hogshead. It is a little hard, that I alone should be unfurnished with a printed copy of this facetious story.

When you visit London next, you must buy the most elegant impression of it, and bring it with you. I thank you also for writing to Johnson. I likewise wrote to him myself. Your letter and mine together have operated to admiration. There needs nothing more but that the effect be lasting, and the whole will soon be printed. We now draw towards the middle of the fifth book of *The Task*. The man, Johnson, is like unto some vicious horses, that I have known. They would not budge till they were spurred, and when they were spurred, they would kick. – So did he; his temper was somewhat disconcerted: but his pace was quickened, and I was contented.

[...]

Your mother and I walked yesterday in the Wilderness. As we entered the gate, a glimpse of something white, contained in a little hole in the gate-post, caught my eye. I looked again, and discovered a bird's nest, with two tiny eggs in it. By and by they will be fledged, and tailed, and get wing-feathers, and fly. My case is somewhat similar to that of the parent bird. My nest is in a little nook. Here I brood and hatch, and in due time my progeny takes wing and whistles.

We wait for the time of your coming with pleasant expectation. – Yours truly,

W.C.

LXIV *To Joseph Hill*   25 June 1785

My Dear Friend,

I write in a nook that I call my *Boudoir*. It is a summerhouse not much bigger than a sedan chair, the door of which opens into the garden, that is now crowded with pinks, roses, and honey-suckles, and the window into my neighbour's orchard. It formerly served an apothecary, now dead, as a smoking-room; and under my feet is a trap-door, which once covered a hole in the ground, where he kept his bottles. At present, however, it is dedicated to sublimer uses. Having lined it with garden mats, and furnished it with a table and two chairs, here

I write all that I write in summer-time, whether to my friends, or to the public. It is secure from all noise, and a refuge from all intrusion; for intruders sometimes trouble me in the winter evenings at Olney. But (thanks to my *Boudoir!*) I can now hide myself from them. A poet's retreat is sacred. They acknowledge the truth of that proposition, and never presume to violate it.

The last sentence puts me in mind to tell you that I have ordered my volume to your door. My bookseller is the most dilatory of all his fraternity, or you would have received it long since. It is more than a month since I returned him the last proof, and consequently since the printing was finished. I sent him the manuscript at the beginning of last November, that he might publish while the town was full; – and he will hit the exact moment when it is entirely empty. Patience (you will perceive) is in no situation exempted from the severest trials; a remark that may serve to comfort you under the numberless trials of your own.

W.C.

LXV *To Lady Hesketh*   12 October 1785

After a break of eighteen years in their correspondence, Cowper received a letter from Harriot Hesketh on 12 October 1785. Lady Hesketh had read 'John Gilpin', and immediately determined to renew their former correspondence. The length and effusiveness of his reply indicates his delight at renewing acquaintance with his cousin.

My Dear Cousin,

It is no new thing with you to give pleasure; but I will venture to say, that you do not often give more than you gave me this morning. When I came down to breakfast, and found upon the table a letter franked by my uncle, and when opening that frank I found that it contained a letter from you, I said within myself – 'This is just as it should be. We are all grown young again, and the days that I thought I should see no more, are actually returned.' You perceive, therefore, that you judged well when you conjectured, that a line from you would not be disagreeable to me. It could not be otherwise than, as in fact it proved, a most agreeable surprise, for I can truly boast of an affection for you, that neither years, nor interrupted intercourse, have at all abated. I need only recollect how much I valued you once, and with how much cause, immediately to feel a revival of the same value: if that can be said to revive, which at the most has only been dormant for want of employment, but I slander it when I say that it has slept. A thousand times have I recollected a thousand scenes, in which our two selves have formed the whole of the drama, with the greatest pleasure; at times, too, when I had no reason to suppose that I should ever hear from you again. I have laughed with you at the *Arabian Nights Entertainment*, which afforded us, as you well know, a fund of merriment that deserves never to be forgot. I have walked with you to Netley Abbey, and have scrambled with you over hedges in every direction, and many other feats we have performed together, upon the field of my remembrance, and all within these few years. Should I say within this twelvemonth, I should not transgress the truth. The hours that I have spent with you were among the pleasantest of my former days, and are therefore chronicled in my mind so deeply, as to feel no erasure. Neither do I forget my poor friend, Sir Thomas. I should remember him, indeed, at any rate, on account of his personal kindness to myself; but the last testimony that he gave of his regard for you endears him to me still more. With his uncommon understanding (for with many peculiarities he had more sense than any of his acquaintance), and with his generous sensibilities, it was hardly possible that he should not distinguish you as he has done. As it was the last, so it was the best proof, that he could give, of a judgement that never deceived him, when he would allow himself leisure to consult it.

You say that you have often heard of me: that puzzles me. I cannot imagine from what quarter, but it is no matter. I must tell you, however, my cousin, that your information has been a little defective. That I am happy in my situation is true; I live, and have lived these twenty years, with Mrs Unwin, to whose affectionate care of me, during the far greater part of that time, it is, under Providence, owing that I live at all. But I do not account myself happy in having been for thirteen of those years in a state of mind that has made all that care and attention necessary; an attention, and a care, that have injured her health, and which, had she not been uncommonly supported, must have brought her to the grave. But I will pass to another subject; it would be cruel to particularize only to give pain, neither would I by any means give a sable hue to the first letter of a correspondence so unexpectedly renewed.

[...]

My dear cousin, dejection of spirits, which, I suppose, may have prevented many a man from becoming an author, made me one. I find constant employment necessary, and therefore take care to be constantly employed. Manual occupations do not engage the mind sufficiently, as I know by experience, having tried many. But composition, especially of verse, absorbs it wholly. I write, therefore, generally three hours in a morning, and in an evening I transcribe. I read also, but less than I write, for I must have bodily exercise, and therefore never pass a day without it.

You ask me where I have been this summer. I answer at Olney. Should you ask me where I spent the last seventeen summers, I should still answer, at Olney. Ay, and the winters also; I have seldom left it, and except when I attended my brother in his last illness, never I believe a fortnight together.

Adieu, my beloved cousin, I shall not always be thus nimble in reply, but shall always have great pleasure in answering you when I can. – Yours, my dear friend, and cousin,

W.C.

LXVI *To Lady Hesketh*   9 November 1785

My Dearest Cousin,
    Whose last most affectionate letter has run in my head ever

since I received it, and which I now sit down to answer two days sooner than the post will serve me; I thank you for it, and with a warmth for which I am sure you will give me credit, though I do not spend many words in describing it; I do not seek *new* friends, not being altogether sure that I should find them, but have unspeakable pleasure in being still beloved by an old one. I hope that now our correspondence has suffered its last interruption, and that we shall go down together to the grave, chatting and chirping as merrily as such a scene of things as this will permit.

I am happy that my poems have pleased you. My volume has afforded me no such pleasure at any time, either, while I was writing it, or since its publication, as I have derived from yours and my uncle's opinion of it. I make certain allowances for partiality, and for that peculiar quickness of taste, with which you both relish what you like, and after all drawbacks upon those accounts duly made, find myself rich in the measure of your approbation that still remains. But above all, I honour John Gilpin, since it was he who first encouraged you to write. I made him on purpose to laugh at, and he served his purpose well; but I am now in debt to him for a more valuable acquisition than all the laughter in the world amounts to, the recovery of my intercourse with you, which is to me inestimable. My benevolent and generous cousin, when I was once asked if I wanted any thing, and given delicately to understand that the inquirer was ready to supply all my occasions, I thankfully and civilly, but positively, declined the favour. I neither suffer, nor have suffered, any such inconveniences as I had not much rather endure than come under obligations of that sort to a person comparatively with yourself a stranger to me. But to you I answer otherwise. I know you thoroughly, and the liberality of your disposition, and have that consummate confidence in the sincerity of your wish to serve me, that delivers me from all awkward constraint, and from all fear of trespassing by acceptance. To you, therefore, I reply, yes. Whensoever, and whatsoever, and in what manner-soever you please; and add moreover, that my affection for the giver is such as will increase to me tenfold the satisfaction that I shall have in receiving. It is necessary, however, that I should let you a little into the state of my finances, that you may not suppose them more narrowly circumscribed than they are. Since Mrs Unwin and I have lived at Olney, we have had but one purse, although during the whole of that time, till lately, her income was nearly double mine. Her revenues indeed are now in some measure reduced, and do not much exceed my own; the worst consequence of this is, that we are forced to deny ourselves some things which hitherto we have been better able to afford, but they are such things as neither life, nor the well-being of life, depend upon. My own income has been better than it is, but when it was best, it would not have enabled me to live as my connexions demanded that I should, had it not been combined with a better than itself, at least at this end of the kingdom. Of this I had full proof during three months that I spent in lodgings at Huntingdon, in which time by the help of good management, and a clear notion of economical matters, I contrived to spend the income of a twelvemonth. Now, my beloved cousin, you are in possession of the whole case as it stands. Strain no points to your own inconvenience or hurt, for there is no need of it, but indulge yourself in communicating (no matter what) that you can spare without missing it, since by so doing you will be sure to add to the comforts of my life one of the sweetest that I can enjoy – a token and proof of your affection.

I cannot believe but that I should know you, notwithstanding all that time may have done: there is not a feature of your face, could I meet it upon the road, by itself, that I should not instantly recollect. I should say, that is my cousin's nose, or those are her lips and her chin, and no woman upon earth can claim them but herself. As for me, I am a very smart youth of my years; I am not indeed grown gray so much as I am grown bald. No matter: there was more hair in the world than ever had the honour to belong to me; accordingly having found just enough to curl a little at my ears, and to intermix with a little of my own, that still hangs behind, I appear, if you see me in an afternoon, to have a very decent head-dress, not easily distinguished from my natural growth, which being worn with a small bag, and a black riband about my neck, continues to me the charms of my youth, even on the verge of age. Away with the fear of writing too often!

W.C.

P.S. – That the view I give you of myself may be complete, I add the two following items – That I am in debt to nobody, and that I grow fat.

LXVII *To John Newton* 3 December 1785

After completing *The Task*, Cowper began to translate Homer's *Iliad* and *Odyssey*, aiming to rival the famous translations from earlier in the century by Alexander Pope. Like Pope, Cowper set out to publish this work by subscription (a process in which the writer's friends and relations, as well as whoever of the great and good could be persuaded, would subscribe to a list of purchasers, thereby guaranteeing sales when the volume finally appeared). While this work was in progress, from 1785 until 1791, it became a major theme of his letters as he began to speculate more rigorously than he had done before about the classics, translation and the nature of art.

My Dear Friend,

[…] For some weeks after I had finished *The Task*, and sent away the last sheet corrected, I was through necessity idle, and suffered not a little in my spirits for being so. One day, being in such distress of mind as was hardly supportable, I took up the *Iliad*; and merely to divert attention, and with no more preconception of what I was then entering upon, than I have at this moment of what I shall be doing this day twenty years hence, translated the twelve first lines of it. The same necessity pressing me again, I had recourse to the same expedient, and translated more. Every day bringing its occasion for employment with it, every day consequently added something to the work; till at last I began to reflect thus: – The *Iliad* and the

Odyssey together consists of about forty thousand verses. To translate these forty thousand verses will furnish me with occupation for a considerable time. I have already made some progress, and I find it a most agreeable amusement. Homer, in point of purity, is a most blameless writer; and, though he was not an enlightened man, has interspersed many great and valuable truths throughout both his poems. In short, he is in all respects a most venerable old gentleman, by an acquaintance with whom no man can disgrace himself. The literati are all agreed to a man, that, although Pope has given us two pretty poems under Homer's titles, there is not to be found in them the least portion of Homer's spirit, nor the least resemblance of his manner. I will try, therefore, whether I cannot copy him somewhat more happily myself. I have at least the advantage of Pope's faults and failings, which, like so many buoys upon a dangerous coast, will serve me to steer by, and will make my chance for success more probable. These and many other considerations, but especially a mind that abhorred a vacuum as its chief bane, impelled me so effectually to the work, that ere long I mean to publish proposals for a subscription to it, having advanced so far as to be warranted in doing so. I have connexions, and no few such, by means of which I have the utmost reason to expect that a brisk circulation may be procured; and if it should prove a profitable enterprise, the profit will not accrue to a man who may be said not to want it. It is a business such as it will not, indeed, lie much in your way to promote; but, among your numerous connexions, it is possible that you may know some who would sufficiently interest themselves in such a work to be not unwilling to subscribe to it. I do not mean – far be it from me – to put you upon making hazardous applications, where you might possibly incur a refusal, that would give you though but a moment's pain. You know best your own opportunities and powers in such a cause. If you can do but little, I shall esteem it much; and if you can do nothing, I am sure that it will not be for want of a will.

[...]

My correspondence has lately also been renewed with my dear cousin Lady Hesketh, whom I ever loved as a sister, (for we were in a manner brought up together,) and who writes to me as affectionately as if she were so. She also enters into my views and interests upon this occasion with a warmth that gives me great encouragement. The circle of her acquaintance is likewise very extensive; and I have no doubt that she will exert her influence to its utmost possibilities among them. I have other strings to my bow, (perhaps, as a translator of Homer, I should say, to my lyre,) which I cannot here enumerate; but, upon the whole, my prospect seems promising enough. I have not yet consulted Johnson upon the occasion, but intend to do it soon.

[...]

The morning is beautiful, and tempts me forth into the garden. It is all the walk that I can have at this season, but not all the exercise. I ring a peal every day upon the dumb-bells.

– I am, my dear friend, most truly, yours and Mrs Newton's,

W.C.

LXVIII *To Lady Hesketh*   15 December 1785

Dearest Cousin,

My desk is always pleasant, but never so pleasant as when I am writing to you. If I am not obliged to you for the thing itself, at least I am for your having decided the matter against me, and resolving that it should come in spite of all my objections. Before it arrived, Mrs Unwin had spied out for it a place that exactly suits it. A certain fly-table in the corner of the room, which I had overlooked, affords it a convenient stand when it is not wanted, and it is easily transferred to a larger when it is. If I must not know to whom I am principally indebted for it, at least let me entreat you to make my acknowledgements of gratitude and love. As to my frequent use of it, I will tell you how that matter stands. When I was writing my first volume, and was but just beginning to emerge from a state of melancholy that had continued some years, (from which, by the way, I do not account myself even now delivered,) Mrs Unwin insisted on my relinquishing the pen, apprehending consequences injurious to my health. When ladies insist, you know, there is an end of the business; obedience on our part becomes necessary. I accordingly obeyed, but having lost my fiddle, I became pensive and unhappy; she therefore restored it to me, convinced of its utility, and from that day to this I have never ceased to scrape. Observe, however, my dear, that I scrape not always. My task that I assign myself is to translate forty lines a day; if they pass off easily I sometimes make them fifty, but never abate any part of the allotted number. Perhaps I am occupied an hour and a half, perhaps three hours; but generally between two and three. This, you see, is labour that can hurt no man; and what I have translated in the morning, in the evening I transcribe.

[...]

With respect to the enterprise itself, there are certain points of delicacy that will not suffer me to make a public justification of it. It would ill become me avowedly to point out the faults of Pope in a preface, and would be as impolitic as indecent. But to you, my dear, I can utter my mind freely. [...] Now for Pope himself: – I will allow his whole merit. He has written a great deal of very musical and sweet verse in his translation of Homer, but his verse is not universally such; on the contrary, it is often lame, feeble, and flat. He has, besides, occasionally a felicity of expression peculiar to himself; but it is a felicity purely modern, and has nothing to do with Homer. Except the Bible, there never was in the world a book so remarkable for that species of the sublime that owes its very existence to simplicity, as the works of Homer. He is always nervous, plain, natural. I refer you to your own knowledge of his copyist for a decision upon Pope's merits in these particulars. The garden in all the gaiety of June is less flowery than his Translation. Metaphors of which Homer never dreamt, which he did not seek, and which probably he would have disdained if he had found, follow each other in quick succession like the sliding pictures in a show box. Homer is, on occasions that call for such a style, the easiest and most familiar of all writers: a circumstance that escaped Pope entirely, who takes most religious care that he shall every where strut in buckram. The speeches of his heroes are often animated to a degree that Pope no doubt accounted unmannerly and rude, for he has reduced numbers of them that are of that character to the perfect standard of French good-breeding. Shakespeare himself did not excel Homer in discrimination of character, neither is he more attentive to exact consistence and preservation of it throughout. In Pope, to whatever cause it was owing, whether he did not see it, or seeing it, accounted it an affair of no moment, this great beauty is almost absolutely annihilated. In short, my dear, there is hardly any thing in the world so unlike another, as Pope's version of Homer to the original. Give me a great corking pin that I may stick your faith upon my sleeve. There – it is done. Now assure yourself, upon the credit of a man who made Homer much his study in his youth, and who is perhaps better acquainted with Pope's translation of him than almost any man, having twenty-five years ago compared them with each other line by line throughout; upon the credit of a man, too, who would not for the world deceive you in the smallest matter, that Pope never entered into the spirit of Homer, that he never translated him, I had almost said, did not understand him: many passages it is literally true that he did not. Why, when he first entered on his task, did he, (as he did, by his own confession,) for ever dream that he was wandering in unknown ways, that he was lost upon heaths and forests, and awoke in terror? I will tell you, my dear, his dreams were emblems of his waking experience; and I am mistaken, if I could not go near to prove that at his first setting out, he knew very little of Greek, and was never an adept in it, to the last. Therefore, my beloved cousin, once more take heart. I have a fair opportunity to acquire honour; and if when I have finished the *Iliad*, I do not upon cool consideration think that I have secured it, I will burn the copy.

[…]

Now farewell, my dearest cousin, and deservedly my most beloved friend, farewell. – With true affection yours,

Wm. Cowper

General Spencer Cowper, the poet's cousin, became interested in the progress of the Homer translation and took an active role in its publication, offering advice and criticism of the poet's progress. Joseph Johnson, having received a specimen of it that was to be published as an abstract, passed it on to the painter Henry Fuseli for his comments. When Fuseli's unsolicited criticisms were seen by Cowper, the poet was so impressed by their acuity that, despite not knowing from where they came, he determined to take on board almost all of the points that were raised. Fuseli became the most influential and incisive assistant for Cowper's translation of *The Iliad*, although by the time Cowper began *The Odyssey* he had lost interest in the project. In a similar manner, Lady Hesketh passed the specimen of Homer to Dr Paul Henry Maty, a librarian at the British Museum and the editor of the *New Review*, for comments which were also to affect the progress of the translation.

[...]

When I write to you, what I have already related to the General, I am always fearful lest I should tell you that for news with which you are well acquainted. For once, however, I will venture. On Wednesday last I received from Johnson the MS. copy of a specimen that I had sent to the General; and, enclosed in the same cover, notes upon it by an unknown critic. Johnson, in a short letter, recommended him to me as a man of unquestionable learning and ability. On perusal and consideration of his remarks, I found him such; and having nothing so much at heart as to give all possible security to yourself and the General, that my work shall not come forth unfinished, I answered Johnson, that I would gladly submit my MS. to his friend. He is in truth a very clever fellow, perfectly a stranger to me, and one who I promise you will not spare for severity of animadversion, where he shall find occasion. It is impossible for you, my dearest cousin, to express a wish that I do not equally feel a wish to gratify. You are desirous that Maty should see a book of my Homer, and for that reason if Maty *will* see a book of it, he shall be welcome, although time is likely to be precious, and consequently any delay, that is not absolutely necessary, as much as possible to be avoided. I am now revising the *Iliad*. It is a business that will cost me four months, perhaps five; for I compare the very words as I go, and if much alteration should occur, must transcribe the whole. The first book I have almost transcribed already. To these five months, Johnson says that nine more must be added for printing, and upon my own experience I will venture to assure you, that the tardiness of printers will make those nine months twelve. There is danger, therefore, that my subscribers may think that I make them wait too long, and that they who know me not, may suspect a bubble. How glad shall I be to read it over in an evening, book by book, as fast as I settle the copy, to you, and to Mrs Unwin! She has been my touchstone always, and without reference to her taste and judgment I have printed nothing. With one of you at each elbow I should think myself the happiest of all poets.

The General and I, having broken the ice, are upon the comfortable terms of correspondence. He writes very affectionately to me, and I say every thing to him that comes uppermost. I could not write frequently to any creature living, upon any other terms than those. He tells me of infirmities that he has, which make him less active than he was. I am sorry to hear that he has any such. Alas! alas! he was young when I saw him only twenty years ago.

[...]

May God have you in his keeping, my beloved cousin! Farewell,

W.C.

LXX *To Lady Hesketh*   9 February 1786

My Dearest Cousin,

I have been impatient to tell you that I am impatient to see you again. Mrs Unwin partakes with me in all my feelings upon this subject, and longs also to see you. I should have told you so by the last post, but have been so completely occupied by this tormenting specimen, that it was impossible to do it. I sent the General a letter on Monday, that would distress and alarm him; I sent him another yesterday, that will, I hope, quiet him again. Johnson has apologized very civilly for the multitude of his friend's strictures; and his friend has promised to confine himself in future to a comparison of me with the original, so that, I doubt not, we shall jog on merrily together. And now, my dear, let me tell you once more, that your kindness in promising us a visit has charmed us both. I shall see you again. I shall hear your voice. We shall take walks together. I will show you my prospects, the hovel, the alcove, the Ouse, and its banks, every thing that I have described. I anticipate the pleasure of those days not very far distant, and feel a part of it at this moment. Talk not of an inn! Mention it not for your life! We have never had so many visitors, but we could easily accommodate them all; though we have received Unwin, and his wife, and his sister, and his son all at once. My dear, I will not let you come till the end of May, or beginning of June, because before that time my greenhouse will not be ready to receive us, and it is the only pleasant room belonging to us. When the plants go out, we go in. I line it with mats, and spread the floor with mats; and there you shall sit with a bed of mignionette at your side, and a hedge of honeysuckles, roses, and jasmine; and I will make you a bouquet of myrtle every day. Sooner than the time I mention the country will not be in complete beauty. And I will tell you what you shall find at your first entrance. Imprimis, as soon as you have entered the vestibule, if you cast a look on either side of you, you shall see on the right hand a box of my making. It is the box in which have been lodged all my hares, and in which lodges Puss at present: but he, poor fellow, is worn out with age, and promises to die before you can see him. On the right hand stands a cupboard, the work of the same author; it was once a dove-cage, but I transformed it. Opposite to you stands a table, which I also made: but a merciless servant having scrubbed it until it became paralytic, it serves no purpose now but of ornament; and all my clean shoes stand under it. On the left hand, at the further end of this superb vestibule, you will find the door of the parlour, into which I will conduct you, and where I will introduce you to Mrs Unwin, unless we should meet her before, and where we will be as happy as the day is long. Order yourself, my cousin, to the Swan at Newport, and there you shall find me ready to conduct you to Olney.

My dear, I have told Homer what you say about casks and urns, and have asked him, whether he is sure that it is a cask in which Jupiter keeps his wine. He swears that it is a cask, and that it will never be any thing better than a cask to eternity. So if the god is content with it, we must even wonder at his taste, and be so too. – Adieu! my dearest, dearest cousin,

W.C.

LXXI *To Lady Hesketh*   29 May 1786

Thou dear, comfortable cousin, whose letters, among all that I receive, have this property peculiarly their own, that I expect them without trembling, and never find any thing in them that does not give me pleasure; for which therefore I would take nothing in exchange that the world could give me, save and except that for which I must exchange them soon, (and happy shall I be to do so,) your own company. That, indeed, is delayed a little too long; to my impatience at least it seems so, who find the spring, backward as it is, too forward, because many of its beauties will have faded before you will have an opportunity to see them. […]

Every day I think of you, and almost all the day long; I will venture to say, that even *you* were never so expected in your life. I called last week at the Quaker's to see the furniture of your bed, the fame of which had reached me. It is, I assure you, superb, of printed cotton, and the subject classical. Every morning you will open your eyes on Phaeton kneeling to Apollo, and imploring his father to grant him the conduct of his chariot for a day. May your sleep be as sound as your bed will be sumptuous, and your nights at least will be well provided for.

I shall send up the sixth and seventh books of the *Iliad* shortly, and shall address them to you. You will forward them to the General. I long to show you my workshop, and to see you sitting on the opposite side of my table. We shall be as close packed as two wax figures in an old fashioned picture frame. I am writing in it now. It is the place in which I fabricate all my verse in summer time. I rose an hour sooner than usual this morning, that I might finish my sheet before breakfast, for I must write this day to the General.

[...]

W.C.

LXXII *To Joseph Hill*

The date given by Southey (19 June 1786) for this letter is incorrect, as Lady Hesketh did not arrive in Olney until 21 June. James King and Charles Ryskamp date the letter 11 July 1786.

My dear cousin's arrival has, as it could not fail to do, made us happier than we ever were at Olney. Her great kindness in giving us her company is a cordial that I shall feel the effect of, not only while she is here, but while I live.

Olney will not be much longer the place of our habitation. At a village two miles distant we have hired a house of Mr Throckmorton, a much better than we occupy at present, and yet not more expensive. It is situated very near to our most agreeable landlord, and his agreeable pleasure grounds. In him, and in his wife, we shall find such companions as will always make the time pass pleasantly while they are in the country, and his grounds will afford us good air, and good walking room in the winter; two advantages which we have not enjoyed at Olney, where I have no neighbour with whom I can converse, and where, seven months in the year, I have been imprisoned by dirty and impassable ways, till both my health and Mrs Unwin's have suffered materially.

Homer is very importunate, and will not suffer me to spend half the time with my distinct friends that I would gladly give them.

W.C.

LXXIII *To William Unwin*   24 August 1786

My Dear Friend,

I catch a minute by the tail and hold it fast, while I write to you. The moment it is fled I must go to breakfast. [...]

I am still occupied in refining and polishing, and shall this morning give the finishing hand to the seventh book. Fuseli does me the honour to say that the most difficult, and most interesting parts of the poem, are admirably rendered. But because he did not express himself equally pleased with the more pedestrian parts of it, my labour therefore has been principally given to the dignification of them; not but that I have retouched considerably, and made better still, the best. In short I hope to make it all of a piece, and shall exert myself to the utmost to secure that desirable point. A storyteller, so very circumstantial as Homer, must of necessity present us often with much matter in itself capable of no other embellishment than purity of diction and harmony of versification can give to it. *Hic labor, hoc opus est.* For our language, unless it be very severely chastised, has not the terseness, nor our measure the music of the Greek. But I shall not fail through want of industry.

We are likely to be very happy in our connexion with the Throckmortons. His reserve and mine wear off, and he talks with great pleasure of the comfort that he proposes to himself from our winter-evening conversations. His purpose seems to be, that we should spend them alternately with each other. Lady Hesketh transcribes for me at present. When she is gone, Mrs Throckmorton takes up that business, and will be my lady of

105

the ink-bottle for the rest of the winter. She solicited herself that office.

[…] – Believe me, my dear William, truly yours,

W.C.

[…]

LXXIV *To Joseph Hill*   6 October 1786

You have not heard, I suppose, that the ninth book of my translation is at the bottom of the Thames. But it is even so. A storm overtook it in its way to Kingston, and it sunk, together with the whole cargo of the boat in which it was a passenger. Not figuratively foreshewing, I hope, by its submersion, the fate of all the rest. My kind and generous cousin, who leaves nothing undone that she thinks can conduce to my comfort, encouragement, or convenience, is my transcriber also. *She* wrote the copy, and *she* will have to write it again, – *Hers*, therefore, is the damage. I have a thousand reasons to lament that the time approaches when we must lose her. She has made a winterly summer a most delightful one, but the winter itself we must spend without her.

W.C.

LXXV *To Walter Bagot*   17 November 1786

On 15 November 1786 Cowper and Mary Unwin moved into the Lodge at Weston Hall in Weston Underwood which they rented from the Throckmortons.

Walter Bagot, one of Cowper's closest friends while he was at Westminster School, became actively involved in hunting out subscribers when he heard about the Homer project.

My Dear Friend,
There are some things that do not actually shorten the life of

man, yet seem to do so, and frequent removals from place to place are of that number. For my own part at least, I am apt to think, if I had been more stationary, I should seem to myself to have lived longer. My many changes of habitation have divided my time into many short periods, and when I look back upon them they appear only as the stages in a day's journey, the first of which is at no very great distance from the last.

I lived longer at Olney than any where. There, indeed, I lived till mouldering walls and a tottering house warned me to depart. I have accordingly taken the hint, and two days since arrived, or rather took up my abode, at Weston. You perhaps have never made the experiment, but I can assure you that the confusion which attends a transmigration of this kind is infinite, and has a terrible effect in deranging the intellects. I have been obliged to renounce my Homer on the occasion, and though not for many days, I yet feel as if study and meditation, so long my confirmed habits, were on a sudden become impracticable, and that I shall certainly find them so when I attempt them again. But in a scene so much quieter and pleasanter than that which I have just escaped from, in a house so much more commodious, and with furniture about me so much more to my taste, I shall hope to recover my literary tendency again, when once the bustle of the occasion shall have subsided.

How glad I should be to receive you under a roof, where you would find me so much more comfortably accommodated than at Olney! I know your warmth of heart toward me, and am sure that you would rejoice in my joy. At present, indeed, I have not had time for much self-gratulation, but have every reason to hope, nevertheless, that in due time I shall derive considerable advantage, both in health and spirits, from the alteration made in my *whereabout*.

I have now the twelfth book of the *Iliad* in hand, having settled the eleven first books finally, as I think, or nearly so. The winter is the time when I make the greatest riddance.

Adieu, my friend Walter. Let me hear from you, and believe me ever yours,

W.C.

It is my birthday, my beloved cousin, and I determine to employ a part of it, that it may not be destitute of festivity, in writing to you. The dark, thick fog that has obscured it, would have been a burthen to me at Olney, but here I have hardly attended to it. The neatness and snugness of our abode compensate all the dreariness of the season, and whether the ways are wet or dry, our house at least is always warm and commodious. Oh for you, my cousin, to partake these comforts with us! I will not begin already to tease you upon that subject, but Mrs Unwin remembers to have heard from your own lips, that you hate London in the spring. Perhaps therefore by that time, you may be glad to escape from a scene which will be every day growing more disagreeable, that you may enjoy the comforts of the lodge. You well know that the best house has a desolate appearance unfurnished. This house accordingly, since it has been occupied by us and our *meubles*, is as much superior to what it was when you saw it, as you can imagine. The parlour is even elegant. When I say that the parlour is elegant, I do not mean to insinuate that the study is not so. It is neat, warm, and silent, and a much better study than I deserve, if I do not produce in it an incomparable translation of Homer. I think every day of those lines of Milton, and congratulate myself on having obtained, before I am quite superannuated, what he seems not to have hoped for sooner:

'And may at length my weary age
Find out the peaceful hermitage!'

For if it is not an hermitage, at least it is a much better thing; and you must always understand, my dear, that when poets talk of cottages, hermitages, and such like things, they mean a house with six sashes in front, two comfortable parlours, a smart staircase, and three bedchambers of convenient dimensions; in short, exactly such a house as this.

The Throckmortons continue the most obliging neighbours in the world. One morning last week, they both went with me to the cliff; – a scene, my dear, in which you would delight beyond measure, but which you cannot visit except in the spring or autumn. The heat of summer, and the clinging dirt of winter would destroy you. What is called the cliff, is no cliff, nor at all like one, but a beautiful terrace, sloping gently down to the Ouse, and from the brow of which, though not lofty, you have a view of such a valley as makes that which you see from the hills near Olney, and which I have had the honour to celebrate, an affair of no consideration.

Wintry as the weather is, do not suspect that it confines me. I ramble daily, and every day change my ramble. Wherever I go, I find short grass under my feet, and when I have travelled perhaps five miles, come home with shoes not at all too dirty for a drawing-room. I was pacing yesterday under the elms, that surround the field in which stands the great alcove, when lifting my eyes I saw two black genteel figures bolt through a hedge into the path where I was walking. You guess already who they were, and that they could be nobody but our neighbours. They had seen me from a hill at a distance, and had traversed a great turnip-field to get at me. You see therefore, my dear, that I am in some request. Alas! in too much request with some people. The verses of Cadwallader have found me at last.

I am charmed with your account of our little cousin at Kensington. If the world does not spoil him hereafter, he will be a valuable man. – Good night, and may God bless thee.

W.C.

LXXVII *To Lady Hesketh*   4 December 1786

On 29 November 1786, William Unwin died suddenly from a fever while visiting his friend Henry Thornton in Winchester.

I sent you, my dear, a melancholy letter, and I do not know that I shall now send you one very unlike it. Not that any thing occurs in consequence of our late loss more afflictive than was to be expected, but the mind does not perfectly recover its tone after a shock like that which has been felt so lately. This I observe, that though my experience has long since taught me, that this world is a world of shadows, and that it is the more prudent, as well as the more Christian course to possess the comforts that we find in it, as if we possessed them not, it is no easy matter to reduce this doctrine into practice. We forget that that God who gave them, may, when he pleases, take them away; and that perhaps it may please him to take them at a time when we least expect, or are least disposed to part from them. Thus it has happened in the present case. There never was a moment in Unwin's life, when there seemed to be more urgent want of him than the moment in which he died. He had attained to an age when, if they are at any time useful, men become useful to their families, their friends, and the world. His parish began to feel, and to be sensible of the advantages of his ministry. The clergy around him were many of them awed by his example. His children were thriving under his own tuition and management, and his eldest boy is likely to feel his loss severely, being by his years in some respect qualified to understand the value of such a parent; by his literary proficiency too clever for a schoolboy, and too young at the same time for the university. The removal of a man in the prime of life of such a character, and with such connexions, seems to make a void in society that can never be filled. God seemed to have made him just what he was, that he might be a blessing to others, and when the influence of his character and abilities began to be felt, removed him. These are mysteries, my dear, that we cannot contemplate without astonishment, but which will nevertheless be explained hereafter, and must in the mean time be revered in silence. It is well for his mother, that she has spent her life in the practice of an habitual acquiescence in the dispensations of Providence, else I know that this stroke would have been heavier, after all that she has suffered upon another account, than she could have borne. She derives, as she well may, great consolation from the thought that he lived the life, and died the death of a Christian. The consequence is, if possible, more unavoidable than the most mathematical conclusion, that therefore he is happy. So farewell, my friend Unwin! the first man

110

for whom I conceived a friendship after my removal from St Alban's, and for whom I cannot but still continue to feel a friendship, though I shall see thee with these eyes no more.

W.C.

LXXVIII *To Walter Bagot*   3 January 1787

My Dear Friend,
    You wish to hear from me at any calm interval of epic frenzy. An interval presents itself, but whether calm or not, is perhaps doubtful. Is it possible for a man to be calm, who for three weeks past has been perpetually occupied in slaughter, – letting out one man's bowels, smiting another through the gullet, transfixing the liver of another, and lodging an arrow in the buttock of a fourth? Read the thirteenth book of the *Iliad*, and you will find such amusing incidents as these the subject of it, the sole subject. In order to interest myself in it, and to catch the spirit of it, I had need discard all humanity. It is woeful work; and were the best poet in the world to give us at this day such a list of killed and wounded, he would not escape universal censure, to the praise of a more enlightened age be it spoken. I have waded through much blood, and through much more I must wade before I shall have finished. I determine in the mean time to account it all very sublime, and for two reasons, – First, because all the learned think so; and secondly, because I am to translate it. But were I an indifferent bystander, perhaps I should venture to wish that Homer had applied his wonderful powers to a less disgusting subject. He has in the *Odyssey*, and I long to get at it.
    I have not the good fortune to meet with any of these fine things, that you say are printed in my praise. But I learn from certain advertisements in the *Morning Herald*, that I make a conspicuous figure in the entertainments of Freemasons' Hall. I learn also that my volumes are out of print, and that a third edition is soon to be published. But if I am not gratified with the sight of odes composed to my honour and glory, I have at least

111

been tickled with some *douceurs* of a very flattering nature by the post. A lady unknown addresses the best of men; – an unknown gentleman has read my inimitable poems, and invites me to his seat in Hampshire; – another incognito gives me hopes of a memorial in his garden, and a Welsh attorney sends me his verses to revise, and obligingly asks,

'Say, shall my little bark attendant sail,
Pursue the triumph, and partake the gale?'

If you find me a little vain hereafter, my friend, you must excuse it, in consideration of these powerful incentives, especially the latter; for surely the poet who can charm an attorney, especially a Welsh one, must be at least an Orpheus, if not something greater.

Mrs Unwin is as much delighted as myself with our present situation. But it is a sort of April-weather life that we lead in this world. A little sunshine is generally the prelude to a storm. Hardly had we begun to enjoy the change, when the death of her son cast a gloom upon every thing. He was a most exemplary man; of your order; learned, polite, and amiable. The father of lovely children, and the husband of a wife (very much like dear Mrs Bagot) who adored him. Adieu, my friend! – Your affectionate

W.C.

LXXIX *To Lady Hesketh*   4 January 1787

The fever that Cowper describes in this letter presaged another bout of insanity. During the first six months of 1787, he lost a great deal of weight and became severely depressed. It has been claimed that, at one point during this depression, Mrs Unwin cut the rope when she found Cowper attempting suicide by hanging himself.

The 'Rose' mentioned in this letter is Samuel Rose, a young lawyer, who quickly became a friend of the poet, and put his legal training to work for Cowper when he negotiated the financial arrangements of the Homer project. Perhaps Rose's most famous client, however, was William Blake whom he defended against a charge of sedition in 1804. The story runs that Rose died from an illness brought on by his exertions in getting Blake acquitted.

I have been so much indisposed with the fever that I told you had seized me, my nights during the whole week may be said to have been almost sleepless. The consequence has been, that except the translation of about thirty lines at the conclusion of the thirteenth book, I have been forced to abandon Homer entirely. This was a sensible mortification to me, as you may suppose, and felt the more because, my spirits of course failing with my strength, I seemed to have peculiar need of my old amusement. It seemed hard therefore to be forced to resign it just when I wanted it most. But Homer's battles cannot be fought by a man who does not sleep well, and who has not some little degree of animation in the day time. Last night, however, quite contrary to my expectations, the fever left me entirely, and I slept quietly, soundly, and long. If it please God that it return not, I shall soon find myself in a condition to proceed. I walk constantly, that is to say, Mrs Unwin and I together; for at these times I keep her continually employed, and never suffer her to be absent from me many minutes. She gives me all her time, and all her attention, and forgets that there is another object in the world.

[...]

My fever is not yet gone, but sometimes seems to leave me. It is altogether of the nervous kind, and attended, now and then, with much dejection.

A young gentleman called here yesterday, who came six miles out of his way to see me. He was on a journey to London from Glasgow, having just left the university there. He came I suppose partly to satisfy his own curiosity, but chiefly, as it seemed, to bring me the thanks of some of the Scotch professors for my two volumes. His name is Rose, an Englishman. Your spirits being good, you will derive more pleasure from this incident than I can at present, therefore I send it. – Adieu, very affectionately,

W.C.

LXXX *To Samuel Rose* 27 August 1787

Dear Sir,

I have not yet taken up the pen again, except to write to you. The little taste that I have had of your company, and your kindness in finding me out, make me wish that we were nearer neighbours, and that there were not so great a disparity in our years; that is to say, not that you were older, but that I were younger. Could we have met in early life, I flatter myself that we might have been more intimate than now we are likely to be. But you shall not find me slow to cultivate such a measure of your regard, as your friends of your own age can spare me. When your route shall lie through this country, I shall hope that the same kindness which has prompted you twice to call on me, will prompt you again, and I shall be happy if, on a future occasion, I may be able to give you a more cheerful reception than can be expected from an invalid. My health and spirits are considerably improved, and I once more associate with my neighbours. My head, however, has been the worst part of me, and still continues so, – is subject to giddiness and pain, maladies very unfavourable to poetical employment; but a preparation of the bark, which I take regularly, has so far been of service to me in those respects, as to encourage in me a hope that by perseverance in the use of it, I may possibly find myself qualified to resume the translation of Homer.

[...]

W.C.

Dear Sir,

A summons from Johnson, which I received yesterday, calls my attention once more to the business of translation. Before I begin I am willing to catch though but a short opportunity to acknowledge your last favour. The necessity of applying myself with all diligence to a long work that has been but too long interrupted, will make my opportunities of writing rare in future.

Air and exercise are necessary to all men, but particularly so to the man whose mind labours; and to him who has been all his life accustomed to much of both, they are necessary in the extreme. My time since we parted, has been devoted entirely to the recovery of health and strength for this service, and I am willing to hope with good effect. Ten months have passed since I discontinued my poetical efforts; I do not expect to find the same readiness as before, till exercise of the neglected faculty, such as it is, shall have restored it to me.

You find yourself, I hope, by this time as comfortably situated in your new abode, as in a new abode one can be. I enter perfectly into all your feelings on occasion of the change. A sensible mind cannot do violence even to a local attachment without much pain. When my father died I was young, too young to have reflected much. He was Rector of Berkhamstead, and there I was born. It had never occurred to me that a parson has no fee-simple in the house and glebe he occupies. There was neither tree, nor gate, nor stile, in all that country, to which I did not feel a relation, and the house itself I preferred to a palace. I was sent for from London to attend him in his last illness, and he died just before I arrived. Then, and not till then, I felt for the first time that I and my native place were disunited for ever. I sighed a long adieu to fields and woods, from which I once thought I should never be parted, and was at no time so sensible of their beauties, as just when I left them all behind me, to return no more.

W.C.

The parliament, my dearest cousin, prorogued continually, is a meteor dancing before my eyes, promising me my wish only to disappoint me, and none but the king and his ministers can tell when you and I shall come together. I hope however that the period, though so often postponed, is not far distant, and that once more I shall behold you, and experience your power to make winter gay and sprightly.

I have a kitten, my dear, the drollest of all creatures that ever wore a cat's skin. Her gambols are not to be described, and would be incredible, if they could. In point of size she is likely to be a kitten always, being extremely small of her age, but time I suppose, that spoils every thing, will make her also a cat. You will see her I hope before that melancholy period shall arrive, for no wisdom that she may gain by experience and reflection hereafter, will compensate the loss of her present hilarity. She is dressed in a tortoise-shell suit, and I know that you will delight in her.

Mrs Throckmorton carries us tomorrow in her chaise to Chicheley. The event however must be supposed to depend on elements, at least on the state of the atmosphere, which is turbulent beyond measure. Yesterday it thundered, last night it lightened, and at three this morning I saw the sky as red as a city in flames could have made it. I have a leech in a bottle that foretells all these prodigies and convulsions of nature: no, not as you will naturally conjecture by articulate utterance of oracular notices, but by a variety of gesticulations, which here I have not room to give an account of. Suffice it to say, that no change of weather surprises him, and that in point of the earliest and most accurate intelligence, he is worth all the barometers in the world. None of them all indeed can make the least pretence to foretell thunder – a species of capacity of which he has given the most unequivocal evidence. I gave but sixpence for him, which is a groat more than the market price, though he is in fact, or rather would be, if leeches were not found in every ditch, an invaluable acquisition.

W.C.

[...]

This morning being the morning of New Year's Day, I sent to the Hall a copy of verses, addressed to Mrs Throckmorton, entitled, the Wish, or the Poet's New Year's Gift. We dine there tomorrow, when, I suppose, I shall hear news of them. Their kindness is so great, and they seize with such eagerness every opportunity of doing all they think will please us, that I held myself almost in duty bound to treat them with this stroke of my profession.

The small pox has done, I believe, all that it has to do at Weston. Old folks, and even women with child, have been inoculated. We talk of our freedom, and some of us are free enough, but not the poor. Dependent as they are upon parish bounty, they are sometimes obliged to submit to impositions, which perhaps in France itself could hardly be paralleled. Can man or woman be said to be free, who is commanded to take a distemper, sometimes at least mortal, and in circumstances most likely to make it so? No circumstance whatever was permitted to exempt the inhabitants of Weston. The old as well as the young have been inoculated. Were I asked, Who is the most arbitrary sovereign on earth? I should answer, neither the king of France, nor the Grand Signior, but an overseer of the poor in England.

I am as heretofore occupied with Homer; my present occupation is the revisal of all I have done, namely of the first fifteen books. I stand amazed at my own increasing dexterity in the business, being verily persuaded that, as far as I have gone, I have improved the work to double its former value.

That you may begin the new year and end it in all health and happiness, and many more when the present shall have been long an old one, is the ardent wish of Mrs Unwin, and of yours, my dearest Coz, most cordially,

W.C.

Cowper's antipathy towards slavery is clear from his earliest poetry. In 'Charity' (from the *Poems*), he states that the 'rights of man' are sacred, and exclaims, 'Nor would [God] endure, that any should control / His freeborn brethren of the southern pole'. Even more powerfully, in Book 2 of *The Task*, he describes slavery as 'human nature's broadest, foulest blot', and urges its abolition. However, in 1788, Cowper became directly involved in fighting for the anti-slavery campaign at the instigation of Newton and Lady Hesketh, writing four ballads against the slave trade: 'The Negro's Complaint', 'Pity for Poor Africans', 'Sweet Meat has Sour Sauce' and 'The Morning Dream'.

Hannah More (1745–1833) was one of the most popular and successful writers of the late eighteenth century. She was a leading campaigner in the anti-slavery movement and, like Cowper, published a series of poems on the subject.

I have now three letters of yours, my dearest cousin, before me, all written in the space of a week, and must be indeed insensible of kindness, did I not feel yours on this occasion. I cannot describe to you, neither could you comprehend it if I should, the manner in which my mind is sometimes impressed with melancholy on particular subjects. Your late silence was such a subject. I heard, saw, and felt a thousand terrible things which had no real existence, and was haunted by them night and day, till they at last extorted from me the doleful epistle, which I have since wished had been burned before I sent it. But the cloud has passed, and as far as you are concerned, my heart is once more at rest.

Before you gave me the hint, I had once or twice, as I lay on my bed, watching the break of day, ruminated on the subject which, in your last but one, you recommended to me.

Slavery, or a release from slavery, such as the poor negroes have endured, or perhaps both these topics together, appeared to me a theme so important at the present juncture, and at the same time so susceptible of poetical management, that I more than once perceived myself ready to start in that career, could I have allowed myself to desert Homer for so long a time as it would have cost me to do them justice.

While I was pondering these things, the public prints informed me that Miss More was on the point of publication, having actually finished what I had not yet begun. The sight of her advertisement convinced me that my best course would be that to which I felt myself most inclined, – to persevere, without turning aside to attend to any other call, however alluring, in the business I have in hand.

It occurred to me likewise, that I have already borne my testimony in favour of my black brethren; and that I was one of the earliest, if not the first, of those who have in the present day expressed their detestation of the diabolical traffic in question.

On all these accounts I judged it best to be silent, and especially because I cannot doubt that some effectual measures will now be taken to alleviate the miseries of their condition, the whole nation being in possession of the case, and it being impossible also to allege an argument in behalf of man-merchandise, that can deserve a hearing. I shall be glad to see Hannah More's poem; she is a favourite writer with me, and has more nerve and energy both in her thoughts and language than half the he rhymers in the kingdom. The *Thoughts on the Manners of the Great* will likewise be most acceptable. I want to learn as much of the world as I can, but to acquire that learning at a distance; and a book with such a title promises fair to serve the purpose effectually.

[…] – Farewell.

W.C.

LXXXV *To Lady Hesketh*   12 March 1788

William Wilberforce (1759–1833) was the parliamentary leader of the movement calling for the abolition of the slave trade. He was not, in fact, the author of *Thoughts on*

the Manners of the Great to General Society (1788), which was
actually written by Hannah More. More's long poem,
Slavery, was also published in 1788.

Slavery, and the Manners of the Great, I have read. The
former I admired, as I do all that Miss More writes, as well for
energy of expression, as for the tendency of the design. I have
never yet seen any production of her pen that has not recommended itself by both these qualifications. There is likewise
much good sense in her manner of treating every subject, and
no mere poetic cant (which is the thing that I abhor) in her
manner of treating any. And this I say, not because you now
know and visit her, but it has long been my avowed opinion of
her works, which I have both spoken and written, as often as I
have had occasion to mention them.

Mr Wilberforce's little book (if he was the author of it) has
also charmed me. It must, I should imagine, engage the notice
of those to whom it is addressed. In that case one may say to
them, either answer it, or be set down by it. They will do neither.
They will approve, commend, and forget it. Such has been the
fate of all exhortations to reform, whether in verse or prose, and
however closely pressed upon the conscience, in all ages. Here
and there a happy individual, to whom God gives grace and
wisdom to profit by the admonition, is the better for it. But the
aggregate body (as Gilbert Cooper used to call the multitude)
remain, though with a very good understanding of the matter,
like horse and mule that have none.

We shall now soon lose our neighbours at the Hall. We shall
truly miss them, and long for their return. Mr Throckmorton
said to me last night, with sparkling eyes, and a face expressive
of the highest pleasure, – 'We compared you this morning with
Pope; we read your fourth *Iliad*, and his, and I verily think we
shall beat him. He has many superfluous lines, and does not
interest one. When I read your translation, I am deeply affected.
I see plainly your advantage, and am convinced that Pope
spoiled all by attempting the work in rhyme.' His brother
George, who is my most active amanuensis, and who indeed
first introduced the subject, seconded all he said. More would

have passed, but Mrs Throckmorton having seated herself at the harpsichord, and for my amusement merely, my attention was of course turned to her. The new vicar of Olney is arrived, and we have exchanged visits. He is a plain, sensible man, and pleases me much. A treasure for Olney, if Olney can understand his value.

W.C.

LXXXVI *To General Spencer Cowper* 1788

The poem enclosed with this letter was 'The Morning Dream'.

My Dear General,

A letter is not pleasant which excites curiosity, but does not gratify it. Such a letter was my last, the defects of which I therefore take the first opportunity to supply. When the condition of our negroes in the islands was first presented to me as a subject for songs, I felt myself not at all allured to the undertaking: it seemed to offer only images of horror, which could by no means be accommodated to the style of that sort of composition. But having a desire to comply, if possible, with the request made to me, after turning the matter in my mind as many ways as I could, I, at last, as I told you, produced three; and that which appears to myself the best of those three I have sent you. Of the other two, one is serious, in a strain of thought perhaps rather too serious, and I could not help it. The other, of which the slave-trader is himself the subject, is somewhat ludicrous. If I could think them worth your seeing, I would, as opportunity should occur, send them also. If this amuses you, I shall be glad.

W.C.

LXXXVII *To Lady Hesketh* 28 July 1788

The reference concerning the 'Five hundred celebrated authors' in this letter is to the anonymously published *Catalogue of Five Hundred Celebrated Authors of Great Britain, Now Living* (1788).

It is in vain that you tell me you have no talent at description, while in fact you describe better than any body. You have given me a most complete idea of your mansion and its situation; and I doubt not that with your letter in my hand by way of map, could I be set down on the spot in a moment, I should find myself qualified to take my walks and my pastime in whatever quarter of your paradise it should please me the most to visit. We also, as you know, have scenes at Weston worthy of description; but because you know them well, I will only say that one of them has, within these few days, been much improved; I mean the lime walk. By the help of the axe and the woodbill, which have of late been constantly employed in cutting out all straggling branches that intercepted the arch, Mr Throckmorton has now defined it with such exactness, that no cathedral in the world can show one of more magnificence or beauty. I bless myself that I live so near it; for were it distant several miles, it would be well worth while to visit it, merely as an object of taste; not to mention the refreshment of such a gloom both to the eyes and spirits. And these are the things which our modern improvers of parks and pleasure grounds have displaced without mercy, because, forsooth, they are rectilinear! It is a wonder they do not quarrel with the sunbeams for the same reason.

Have you seen the account of Five hundred celebrated authors now living? I am one of them; but stand charged with the high crime and misdemeanor of totally neglecting method; an accusation which, if the gentleman would take the pains to read me, he would find sufficiently refuted. I am conscious at least myself of having laboured much in the arrangement of my matter, and of having given to the several parts of my book of *The Task*, as well as to each poem in the first volume, that sort of slight connexion which poetry demands; for in poetry, (except professedly of the didactic kind) a logical precision would be stiff, pedantic, and ridiculous. But there is no pleasing some critics; the comfort is, that I am contented, whether they be pleased or not. At the same time, to my honour be it spoken, the chronicler of us five hundred prodigies bestows on me, for aught I know, more commendations than on any other of my confraternity. May he live to write the histories of as many thousand poets, and find me the very best among them! Amen!

I join with you, my dearest coz, in wishing that I owned the fee simple of all the beautiful scenes around you, but such emoluments were never designed for poets. Am I not happier than ever poet was, in having thee for my cousin, and in the expectation of thy arrival here whenever Strawberry Hill shall lose thee? – Ever thine,

W.C.

LXXXVIII *To Samuel Rose*   1788

This letter, first printed by William Hayley in his *The Life and Posthumous Writings of William Cowper* (1803–4), is a conflation of two letters: the first two paragraphs from 25 September and, according to King and Ryskamp in *The Letters and Prose Writings of William Cowper*, the final one from a letter to Rose dated 11 November. The poem that Cowper proposes at the end of this letter finally appeared as the mock-epic, 'On the Death of Mrs (Now Lady) Throckmorton's Bullfinch' in 1789.

My Dear Friend,

[...] The half hour next before breakfast I devote to you. The moment Mrs Unwin arrives in the study, be what I have written much or little, I shall make my bow, and take leave. If you live to be a judge, as if I augur right you will, I shall expect to hear of a walking circuit.

[...]

I rejoice that you are prepared for transcript work: here will be plenty for you. The day on which you shall receive this, I beg you will remember to drink one glass, at least, to the success of the *Iliad*, which I finished the day before yesterday, and yesterday began the *Odyssey*. It will be some time before I shall perceive myself travelling in another road; the objects around me are at present so much the same, Olympus and a council of

123

gods meet me at my first entrance. To tell you the truth, I am weary of heroes and deities, and, with reverence be it spoken, shall be glad, for variety's sake, to exchange their company for that of a Cyclops.

Weston has not been without its tragedies since you left us: Mrs Throckmorton's piping bullfinch has been eaten by a rat, and the villain left nothing but poor Bully's beak behind him. It will be a wonder if this event does not at some convenient time employ my versifying passion. Did ever fair lady, from the Lesbia of Catullus to the present day, lose her bird, and find no poet to commemorate the loss?

W.C.

LXXXIX *To John Newton*   16 August 1789

My Dear Friend,

Mrs Newton and you are both kind and just in believing that I do not love you less when I am long silent. Perhaps a friend of mine, who wishes me to have him always in my thoughts, is never so effectually possessed of the accomplishment of that wish, as when I have been long his debtor; for *then* I think of him not only every day, but day and night, and all day long. But I confess at the same time, that my thoughts of you will be more pleasant to myself when I shall have exonerated my conscience by giving you the letter so long your due. Therefore, here it comes; – little worth your having; but payment such as it is, that you have a right to expect, and that is essential to my own tranquillity.

That the *Iliad* and the *Odyssey* should have proved the occasion of my suspending my correspondence with you, is a proof how little we foresee the consequences of what we publish. Homer, I dare say, hardly at all suspected that at the fag-end of time two personages would appear, the one ycleped Sir Newton, and the other Sir Cowper, who loving each other heartily, would nevertheless suffer the pains of an interrupted intercourse, his poems the cause. So, however, it has happened;

and though it would not, I suppose, extort from the old bard a single sigh, if he knew it, yet to me it suggests the serious reflection above mentioned. An author by profession had need narrowly to watch his pen, lest a line should escape it which by possibility may do mischief, when he has been long dead and buried. What we have done, when we have written a book, will never be known till the day of judgement: then the account will be liquidated, and all the good that it has occasioned, and all the evil, will witness either for or against us.

I am now in the last book of the *Odyssey*, yet have still, I suppose, half a year's work before me. The accurate revisal of two such voluminous poems can hardly cost me less. I rejoice, however, that the goal is in prospect; for though it has cost me years to run this race, it is only now that I begin to have a glimpse of it. That I shall never receive any proportionable pecuniary recompense for my long labours, is pretty certain; and as to any fame that I may possibly gain by it, *that* is a commodity that daily sinks in value, in measure as the consummation of all things approaches. In the day when the lion shall dandle the kid, and a little child shall lead them, the world will have lost all relish for the fabulous legends of antiquity, and Homer and his translator may budge off the stage together.

The ladies are coming down, and breakfast is at hand. Should I throw aside my letter unfinished, it is not probable that I shall be able to send it by this opportunity. Therefore that you may not wait longer for that for which you have waited too long already, I will only add that I always love and value you both as much as you can possibly wish, and that I am, with Mrs Unwin's affectionate remembrances, my dear friend, ever yours,
                                                              Wm. Cowper

You know that Lady Hesketh is with us; you have had her compliments before, and I send them now, because she would bid me, if she knew that I write to you. We have a snug summer. Our neighbours are out on a ramble, and we have all their pleasant places to ourselves. Not that their return in September will interrupt our pleasures, for they are kind and agreeable, but it will give them a different cast.

My Dear Friend,

The hamper is come, and come safe; and the contents I can affirm on my own knowledge are excellent. It chanced that another hamper and a box came by the same conveyance, all which I unpacked and expounded in the hall; my cousin sitting, mean time, on the stairs, spectatress of the business. We diverted ourselves with imagining the manner in which Homer would have described the scene. Detailed in his circumstantial way, it would have furnished materials for a paragraph of considerable length in an *Odyssey*.

> The straw-stuff'd hamper with his ruthless steel
> He open'd, cutting sheer th' inserted cords,
> Which bound the lid and lip secure. Forth came
> The rustling package first, bright straw of wheat,
> Or oats, or barley, next a bottle green
> Throat-full, clear spirits the contents, distill'd
> Drop after drop odorous, by the art
> Of the fair mother of his friend – the Rose.

And so on. I should rejoice to be the hero of such a tale in the hands of Homer.

You will remember, I trust, that when the state of your health or spirits calls for rural walks and fresh air, you have always a retreat at Weston.

We are all well, all love you, down to the very dog; and shall be glad to hear that you have exchanged languor for alacrity, and the debility that you mention, for indefatigable vigour.

Mr Throckmorton has made me a handsome present: Villoisin's edition of the *Iliad*, elegantly bound by Edwards. If I live long enough, by the contributions of my friends I shall once more be possessed of a library. – Adieu,

W.C.

On 14 July 1789, an angry mob stormed the Bastille prison in Paris, thereby setting the French Revolution in train.

My Dear Friend,

The present appears to me a wonderful period in the history of mankind. That nations so long contentedly slaves should on a sudden become enamoured of liberty, and understand, as suddenly, their own natural right to it, feeling themselves at the same time inspired with resolutions to assert it, seems difficult to account for from natural causes. With respect to the final issue of all this, I can only say, that if, having discovered the value of liberty, they should next discover the value of peace, and lastly the value of the word of God, they will be happier than they ever were since the rebellion of the first pair, and as happy as it is possible they should be in the present life. – Most sincerely yours,

W.C.

The 'Mrs Bodham', to whom this letter is addressed is Anne Bodham (*née* Donne), Cowper's cousin. On hearing of the poet's success from her nephew, John Johnson, she sent Cowper a miniature portrait of his long-dead mother, a gift that thrilled him immensely. In January 1790, John Johnson had introduced himself to Cowper at Weston, and the two immediately struck up a warm and lasting friendship.

The references to the 'Dean of St Paul's' in this letter are to the poet John Donne who (at least according to conjecture) was an ancestor of Cowper on his mother's side of the family.

My Dearest Rose,

Whom I thought withered, and fallen from the stalk, but whom I find still alive: nothing could give me greater pleasure than to know it, and to learn it from yourself. I loved you dearly when you were a child, and love you not a jot the less for having ceased to be so. Every creature that bears any affinity to my mother is dear to me, and you, the daughter of her brother, are but one remove distant from her: I love you, therefore, and love you much, both for her sake, and for your own. The world could not have furnished you with a present so acceptable to me, as the picture which you have so kindly sent me. I received it the night before last, and viewed it with a trepidation of nerves and spirits somewhat akin to what I should have felt, had the dear original presented herself to my embraces. I kissed it, and hung it where it is the last object that I see at night, and, of course, the first on which I open my eyes in the morning. She died when I completed my sixth year; yet I remember her well, and am an ocular witness of the great fidelity of the copy. I remember, too, a multitude of the maternal tendernesses which I received from her, and which have endeared her memory to me beyond expression. There is in me, I believe more of the Donne than of the Cowper; and though I love all of both names, and have a thousand reasons to love those of my own name, yet I feel the bond of nature draw me vehemently to your side. I was thought in the days of my childhood much to resemble my mother; and in my natural temper, of which at the age of fifty-eight I must be supposed to be a competent judge, can trace both her, and my late uncle, your father. Somewhat of his irritability; and a little, I would hope, both of his and of her – , I know not what to call it, without seeming to praise myself, which is not my intention, but speaking to *you*, I will even speak out, and say *good nature*. Add to all this, I deal much in poetry, as did our venerable ancestor, the Dean of St. Paul's, and I think I shall have proved myself a Donne at all points. The truth is, that whatever I am, I love you all.

I account it a happy event that brought the dear boy, your nephew, to my knowledge; and that breaking through all the restraints which his natural bashfulness imposed on him, he

128

determined to find me out. He is amiable to a degree that I have seldom seen, and I often long with impatience to see him again.

[...]

I am much obliged to Mr Bodham for his kindness to my Homer, and with my love to you all, and with Mrs Unwin's kind respects, am, my dear, dear Rose, ever yours,

W.C.

[...]

XCIII *To Lady Hesketh*   22 March 1790

The manuscript of the translation that was lost (see letter LXXIV), was recovered from the bottom of the Thames, which Cowper saw as auguring success for his project.

I rejoice, my dearest cousin, that my MSS. have roamed the earth so successfully, and have met with no disaster. The single book excepted that went to the bottom of the Thames and rose again, they have been fortunate without exception. I am not superstitious, but have nevertheless as good a right to believe that adventure an omen, and a favourable one, as Swift had to interpret, as he did, the loss of a fine fish, which he had no sooner laid on the bank, than it flounced into the water again. This he tells us himself he always considered as a type of his future disappointments: and why may not I as well consider the marvellous recovery of my lost book from the bottom of the Thames, as typical of its future prosperity? To say the truth, I have no fears now about the success of my Translation, though in time past I have had many. I knew there was a style some-where, could I but find it, in which Homer ought to be rendered, and which alone would suit him. Long time I blundered about it, ere I could attain to any decided judgement on the matter; at first I was betrayed by a desire of accommodating my language to the simplicity of his, into much of the quaintness that belonged to our writers of the fifteenth century. In the course of

129

many revisals I have delivered myself from this evil, I believe, entirely; but I have done it slowly, and as a man separates himself from his mistress when he is going to marry. I had so strong a predilection in favour of this style at first, that I was crazed to find that others were not as much enamoured with it as myself. At every passage of that sort which I obliterated, I groaned bitterly, and said to myself, I am spoiling my work to please those who have no taste for the simple graces of antiquity. But in measure, as I adopted a more modern phraseology, I became a convert to their opinion, and in the last revisal, which I am now making, am not sensible of having spared a single expression of the obsolete kind. I see my work so much improved by this alteration, that I am filled with wonder at my own backwardness to assent to the necessity of it, and the more when I consider that Milton, with whose manner I account myself intimately acquainted, is never quaint, never twangs through the nose, but is every where grand and elegant, without resorting to musty antiquity for his beauties. On the contrary, he took a long stride forward, left the language of his own day far behind him, and anticipated the expressions of a century yet to come.

I have now, as I said, no longer any doubt of the event, but I will give thee a shilling if thou wilt tell me what I shall say in my Preface. It is an affair of much delicacy, and I have as many opinions about it as there are whims in a weathercock.

Send my MSS. and thine when thou wilt. In a day or two I shall enter on the last *Iliad*. When I have finished it I shall give the *Odyssey* one more reading, and shall therefore shortly have occasion for the copy in thy possession; but you see that there is no need to hurry.

[...]

W.C.

Your MSS. arrived safe in New Norfolk Street, and I am much obliged to you for your labours. Were you now at Weston I could furnish you with employment for some weeks, and shall perhaps be equally able to do it in summer, for I have lost my best amanuensis in this place, Mr George Throckmorton, who is gone to Bath.

You are a man to be envied, who have never read the *Odyssey*, which is one of the most amusing storybooks in the world. There is also much of the finest poetry in the world to be found in it, notwithstanding all that Longinus has insinuated to the contrary. His comparison of the *Iliad* and *Odyssey* to the meridian, and to the declining sun, is pretty, but I am persuaded, not just The prettiness of it seduced him; he was otherwise too judicious a reader of Homer to have made it. I can find in the latter no symptoms of impaired ability, none of the effects of age; on the contrary, it seems to me a certainty, that Homer, had he written the *Odyssey* in his youth, could not have written it better: and if the *Iliad* in his old age, that he would have written it just as well. A critic would tell me, that instead of written, I should have said *composed*. Very likely; – but I am not writing to one of that snarling generation.

My boy, I long to see thee again. It has happened some way or other, that Mrs Unwin and I have conceived a great affection for thee. That I should, is the less to be wondered at, (because thou art a shred of my own mother;) neither is the wonder great that she should fall into the same predicament: for she loves every thing that I love. You will observe, that your own personal right to be beloved makes no part of the consideration. There is nothing that I touch with so much tenderness as the vanity of a young man, because I know how extremely susceptible he is of impressions that might hurt him in that particular part of his composition. If you should ever prove a coxcomb, from which character you stand just now at a greater distance than any young man I know, it shall never be said that I have made you one; no, you will gain nothing by me but the honour of being much valued by a poor poet, who can do you no good while he lives, and has nothing to leave you when he dies. If you can be contented to be dear to me on these conditions, so you shall; but other terms more advantageous than these, or more inviting, none have I to propose.

Farewell. Puzzle not yourself about a subject when you write to either of us; every thing is subject enough from those we love.

W.C.

XCV *To Lady Hesketh* 28 May 1790

The death of the Poet Laureate, Thomas Warton, in 1790 left that position vacant. A number of Cowper's friends urged that his name be put forward, but he declined their offers. In the event, Warton was succeeded by Henry James Pye, a singularly undistinguished holder of the post who was very much the safe political appointment in a period of major upheaval. Lord Byron, in his usual forthright style, would later describe Pye as 'eminently respectable in everything but his poetry'.

My Dearest Coz,

I thank thee for the offer of thy best services on this occasion. But Heaven guard my brows from the wreath you mention, whatever wreath beside may hereafter adorn them! It would be a leaden extinguisher clapped on all the fire of my genius, and I should never more produce a line worth reading. To speak seriously, it would make me miserable, and therefore I am sure that thou, of all my friends, wouldst least wish me to wear it. Adieu, ever thine, – in Homer-hurry,

W. C.

Instead of beginning with the saffron-vested morning to which Homer invites me, on a morning that has no saffron vest to boast, I shall begin with you.

It is irksome to us both to wait so long as we must for you, but we are willing to hope that by a longer stay you will make us amends for all this tedious procrastination.

Mrs Unwin has made known her whole case to Mr Gregson, whose opinion of it has been very consolatory to me: he says indeed it is a case perfectly out of the reach of all physical aid, but at the same time not at all dangerous. Constant pain is a sad grievance, whatever part is affected, and she is hardly ever free from an aching head, as well as an uneasy side, but patience is an anodyne of God's own preparation, and of that he gives her largely.

The French, who like all lively folks are extreme in every thing, are such in their zeal for freedom; and if it were possible to make so noble a cause ridiculous, their manner of promoting it could not fail to do so. Princes and peers reduced to plain gentlemanship, and gentles reduced to a level with their own lackeys, are excesses of which they will repent hereafter. Differences of rank and subordination are, I believe, of God's appointment, and consequently essential to the well-being of society: but what we mean by fanaticism in religion is exactly that which animates their politics; and unless time should sober them, they will, after all, be an unhappy people. Perhaps it deserves not much to be wondered at, that at their first escape from tyrannic shackles they should act extravagantly, and treat their kings as they have sometimes treated their idols. To these however they are reconciled in due time again, but their respect for monarchy is at an end. They want nothing now but a little English sobriety, and that they want extremely: I heartily wish them some wit in their anger, for it were great pity that so many millions should be miserable for want of it.

My Dear Friend,

Your letter was particularly welcome to me, not only because it came after a long silence, but because it brought me good news – news of your marriage, and consequently, I trust, of your happiness. May that happiness be durable as your lives, and may you be the *Felices ter et amplius* of whom Horace sings so sweetly! This is my sincere wish, and, though expressed in prose, shall serve as your epithalamium. You comfort me when you say that your marriage will not deprive us of the sight of you hereafter. If you do not wish that I should regret your union, you must make that assurance good as often as you have opportunity.

After perpetual versification during five years, I find myself at last a vacant man, and reduced to read for my amusement. My Homer is gone to the press, and you will imagine that I feel a void in consequence. The proofs, however, will be coming soon, and I shall avail myself, with all my force, of this last opportunity, to make my work as perfect as I wish it. I shall not, therefore, be long time destitute of employment, but shall have sufficient to keep me occupied all the winter, and part of the ensuing spring, for Johnson purposes to publish either in March, April, or May. My very preface is finished; it did not cost me much trouble, being neither long nor learned. I have spoken my mind as freely as decency would permit on the subject of Pope's version, allowing him, at the same time, all the merit to which I think him entitled. I have given my reasons for translating in blank verse, and hold some discourse on the mechanism of it, chiefly with a view to obviate the prejudices of some people against it. I expatiate a little on the manner in which I think Homer ought to be rendered, and in which I have endeavoured to render him myself, and anticipated two or three cavils, to which I foresee that I shall be liable from the ignorant, or uncandid, in order, if possible, to prevent them. These are the chief heads of my preface, and the whole consists of about twelve pages.

It is possible when I come to treat with Johnson about the

copy, I may want some person to negotiate for me; and knowing no one so intelligent as yourself in books, or so well qualified to estimate their just value, I shall beg leave to resort to and rely on you as my negotiator. But I will not trouble you unless I should see occasion. My cousin was the bearer of my MSS. to London: he went on purpose, and returns tomorrow. Mrs Unwin's affectionate felicitations, added to my own, conclude me, my dear friend, sincerely yours,

W.C.

XCVIII *To Joseph Hill*   17 September 1790

My Dear Friend,

I received last night a copy of my subscribers' names from Johnson, in which I see how much I have been indebted to yours and Mrs Hill's solicitations. Accept my best thanks, so justly due to you both. It is an illustrious catalogue, in respect of rank and title; but methinks I should have liked it as well had it been more numerous. The sum subscribed, however, will defray the expense of printing; which is as much as, in these unsubscribing days, I had any reason to promise myself. I devoutly second your droll wish, that the booksellers may contend about me. The more the better. Seven times seven, if they please; and let them fight with the fury of Achilles,

Till every rubric-post be crimson'd o'er
With blood of booksellers, in battle slain,
For me, and not a periwig untorn.

– Most truly yours,

Wm. Cowper

My Dear Friend,

I forget if I told you that Mr Throckmorton had applied through the medium of —— to the university of Oxford. He did so, but without success. Their answer has, 'that they subscribe to nothing.'

Pope's subscriptions did not amount, I think, to six hundred; and mine will not fall very short of five. Noble doings, at a time of day when Homer has no news to tell us, and when all other comforts of life having arisen in price, poetry has of course fallen. I call it a 'comfort of life': it is so to others, but to myself, it is become even a necessary.

These holiday times are very unfavourable to the printer's progress. He and all his demons are making themselves merry, and me sad, for I mourn at every hinderance.

W.C.

C *To Lady Hesketh*   18 May 1791

My Dearest Coz
[...]
I have had a letter lately from New York, from a Dr Cogswell of that place, to thank me for my fine verses, and to tell me, which pleased me particularly, that after having read *The Task*, my first volume fell into his hands, which he read also, and was equally pleased with. This is the only instance I can recollect of a reader who has done justice to my first effusions: for I am sure, that in point of expression they do not fall a jot below my second, and that in point of subject they are for the most part superior. But enough, and too much of this. *The Task* he tells me has been reprinted in that city. – Adieu! my dearest coz.

We have blooming scenes under wintry skies, and with icy blasts to fan them. – Ever thine,

W.C.

Dear Sir,

Your letter and obliging present from so great a distance, deserved a speedier acknowledgment, and should not have wanted one so long, had not circumstances so fallen out since I received them as to make it impossible for me to write sooner. It is indeed but within this day or two that I have heard how, by the help of my bookseller, I may transmit an answer to you.

My title page, as it well might, misled you. It speaks me of the Inner Temple, and so I am, but a member of that society only, not as an inhabitant. I live here, almost at the distance of sixty miles from London, which I have not visited these eight-and-twenty years, and probably never shall again. Thus it fell out, that Mr Morewood had sailed again for America before your parcel reached me, nor should I (it is likely) have received it at all, had not a cousin of mine, who lives in the Temple, by good fortune received it first, and opened your letter; finding for whom it was intended, he transmitted to me both that and the parcel. Your testimony of approbation of what I have published, coming from another quarter of the globe, could not be but extremely flattering, as was your obliging notice, that the *Task* had been reprinted in your city. Both volumes, I hope, have a tendency to discountenance vice, and promote the best interests of mankind. But how far they shall be effectual to these invaluable purposes, depends altogether on His blessing, whose truths I have endeavoured to inculcate. In the meantime I have sufficient proof that readers may be pleased, may approve, and yet lay down the book unedified.

During the last five years I have been occupied with a work of a very different nature, a translation of the *Iliad* and *Odyssey* into blank verse, and the work is now ready for publication. I undertook it, partly because Pope's is too lax a version, which has lately occasioned the learned of this country to call aloud for a new one, and partly because I could fall on no better expedient to amuse a mind too much addicted to melancholy.

[...]

I shall account a correspondence with you an honour, and remain, dear sir, your obliged and obedient servant,

W.C.

CII *To John Johnson* 9 August 1791

My Dearest Johnny,

The little that I have heard about Homer myself has been equally, or more flattering than Dr ——'s intelligence, so that I have good reason to hope that I have not studied the old Grecian, and how to dress him, so long, and so intensely, to no purpose. At present I am idle, both on account of my eyes, and because I know not to what to attach myself in particular. Many different plans and projects are recommended to me. Some call aloud for original verse, others for mere translation, and others for other things. Providence, I hope, will direct me in my choice; for other guide I have none, nor wish for another.

God bless you, my dearest Johnny.

W.C.

CIII *To Samuel Rose* 21 December 1791

My Dear Friend,

It grieves me, after having indulged a little hope that I might see you in the holidays, to be obliged to disappoint myself. The occasion too is such as will ensure me your sympathy.

On Saturday last, while I was at my desk near the window, and Mrs Unwin at the fireside, opposite to it, I heard her suddenly exclaim, 'Oh! Mr Cowper, don't let me fall!' I turned and saw her actually falling, together with her chair, and started to her side just in time to prevent her. She was seized with a violent giddiness, which lasted, though with some abatement, the whole day, and was attended too with some other very, very alarming symptoms. At present however she is relieved from the vertigo, and seems in all respects better.

She has been my faithful and affectionate nurse for many years, and consequently has a claim on all my attentions. She has them, and will have them as long as she wants them; which will probably be, at the best, a considerable time to come. I feel the shock, as you may suppose, in every nerve. God grant that there may be no repetition of it. Another such a stroke upon her would, I think, overset me completely; but at present I hold up bravely.

W.C.

CIV *To William Hayley*   6 April 1792

In 1791, Cowper was commissioned by Joseph Johnson to provide the annotation for a new edition of Milton's work that was to be illustrated by Fuseli. When this edition was announced, it provoked William Hayley, who had been approached to perform a similar task by a rival publisher, to contact Cowper. Hayley was a poet, essayist and dramatist, and one of the foremost men-of-letters of the period. Once the two writers established contact, they became firm friends and frequent correspondents.

God grant that this friendship of ours may be a comfort to us all the rest of our days, in a world where true friendships are rarities, and especially where suddenly formed they are apt soon to terminate! But, as I said before, I feel a disposition of heart toward you that I never felt for one whom I had never seen; and that shall prove itself, I trust, in the event a propitious omen.

[…]

It gives me the sincerest pleasure that I may hope to see you at Weston; for as to any migrations of mine, they must, I fear, notwithstanding the joy I should feel in being a guest of yours, be still considered in the light of impossibilities. Come then, my friend, and be as welcome, as the country people say here, as the flowers in May! I am happy, as I say, in the expectation; but the fear, or rather the consciousness that I shall not answer on a nearer view, makes it a trembling kind of happiness, and a doubtful.

After the privacy which I have mentioned above, I went to Huntingdon; soon after my arrival there, I took up my quarters at the house of the Rev. Mr Unwin; I lived with him while he lived, and ever since his death have lived with his widow. Her, therefore, you will find mistress of the house; and I judge of you amiss, or you will find her just such as you would wish. To me she has been often a nurse, and invariably the kindest friend through a thousand adversities that I have had to grapple with in the course of almost thirty years. I thought it better to introduce her to you thus, than to present her to you at your coming, quite a stranger.

Bring with you any books that you think may be useful to my commentatorship, for with you for an interpreter I shall be afraid of none of them. And in truth, if you think that you shall want them, you must bring books for your own use also, for they are an article with which I am *heinously unprovided*; being much in the condition of the man whose library Pope describes as

No mighty store,
His own works neatly bound, and little more!

You shall know how this has come to pass hereafter.

Tell me, my friend, are your letters in your own handwriting? If so, I am in pain for your eyes, lest by such frequent demands upon them I should hurt them. I had rather write you three letters for one, much as I prize your letters, than *that* should happen. And now for the present, adieu; – I am going to accompany Milton into the lake of fire and brimstone, having just begun my annotations.

W.C.

Mary Unwin had suffered bouts of ill health for some years, but during Hayley's first visit to Cowper, things took a turn for the worse. On 22 May 1792 she suffered a severe stroke.

I wish with all my heart, my dearest coz, that I had not ill news for the subject of the present letter. My friend, my Mary, has again been attacked by the same disorder that threatened me last year with the loss of her, and of which you were yourself a witness. Gregson would not allow that first stroke to be paralytic, but this he acknowledges to be so; and with respect to the former, I never had myself any doubt that it was; but this has been much the severest. Her speech has been almost unintelligible from the moment that she was struck; it is with difficulty that she opens her eyes, and she cannot keep them open, the muscles necessary to the purpose being contracted; and as to self-moving powers, from place to place, and the use of her right hand and arm, she has entirely lost them.

It has happened well, that of all men living the man most qualified to assist and comfort me is here, though till within these few days I never saw him, and a few weeks since had no expectation that I ever should. You have already guessed that I mean Hayley. Hayley who loves me as if he had known me from my cradle. When he returns to town, as he must, alas! too soon, he will pay his respects to you.

I will not conclude without adding that our poor patient is beginning, I hope, to recover from this stroke also; but her amendment is slow, as must be expected at her time of life and in such a disorder. I am as well myself as you have ever known me in a time of much trouble, and even better.

It was not possible to prevail on Mrs Unwin to let me send for Dr Kerr, but Hayley has written to his friend Dr Austin a representation of her case, and we expect his opinion and advice tomorrow. In the mean time, we have borrowed an electrical machine from our neighbour Socket, the effect of which she tried yesterday, and the day before, and we think it has been of material service.

She was seized while Hayley and I were walking, and Mr Greatheed, who called while we were absent, was with her.

I forgot in my last to thank thee for the proposed amendments of thy friend. Whoever he is, make my compliments to him, and thank him. The passages to which he objects have been all altered; and when he shall see them new dressed, I hope he will like them better.

W.C.

CVI *To William Hayley* 4 June 1792

ALL'S WELL;

Which words I place as conspicuously as possible, and prefix them to my letter, to save you the pain, my friend and brother, of a moment's anxious speculation. Poor Mary proceeds in her amendment still, and improves, I think, even at a swifter rate than when you left her. The stronger she grows, the faster she gathers strength, which is perhaps the natural course of recovery. She walked so well this morning, that she told me at my first visit she had entirely forgot her illness; and she spoke so distinctly, and had so much of her usual countenance, that, had it been possible, she would have made me forget it too.

Returned from my walk, blown to tatters – found two dear things in the study, your letter, and my Mary! She is bravely well, and your beloved epistle does us both good. I found your kind pencil note in my song-book, as soon as I came down on the morning of your departure; and Mary was vexed to the heart, that the simpletons who watched her supposed her asleep, when she was not; for she learned soon after you were gone, that you would have peeped at her, had you known her to have been awake. I perhaps might have had a peep too, and therefore was as vexed as she; but if it please God, we shall make ourselves large amends for all lost peeps by and by at Eartham.

W.C.

> Through floods and flames to your retreat
>> I win my desperate way,
> And when we meet, if e'er we meet,
>> Will echo your huzza!

You will wonder at the word *desperate* in the second line, and at the *if* in the third; but could you have any conception of the fears I have had to battle with, of the dejection of spirits that I have suffered concerning this journey, you would wonder much more that I still courageously persevere in my resolution to undertake it. Fortunately for my intentions, it happens, that as the day approaches my terrors abate; for had they continued to be what they were a week since, I must, after all, have disappointed you; and was actually once on the verge of doing it. I have told you something of my nocturnal experiences, and assure you now, that they were hardly ever more terrific than on this occasion. Prayer has, however, opened my passage at last, and obtained for me a degree of confidence, that I trust will prove a comfortable viaticum to me all the way. On Wednesday, therefore, we set forth.

The terrors that I have spoken of, would appear ridiculous to most; but to you they will not, for you are a reasonable creature, and know well, that to whatever cause it be owing (whether to constitution, or to God's express appointment), I am hunted by spiritual hounds in the night season. I cannot help it. You will pity me, and wish it were otherwise; and though you may think there is much of the imaginary in it, will not deem it for that reason an evil less to be lamented. So much for fears and distresses. Soon I hope they shall all have a joyful termination, and I, my Mary, my Johnny, and my dog, be skipping with delight at Eartham.

[...]

I hope, or rather, wish, that at Eartham I may recover that habit of study, which, inveterate as it once seemed, I now seem to have lost, – lost to such a degree, that it is even painful to me to think of what it will cost me to acquire it again.

Adieu! my dear, dear Hayley; God give us a happy meeting! Mary sends her love. She is in pretty good plight this morning, having slept well, and for her part, has no fears at all about the journey. – Ever yours,

W.C.

CVIII *To Samuel Greatheed*   6 August 1792

On 3 August 1792 Cowper, Mrs Unwin and a party of their friends including John Johnson arrived at Hayley's residence in Eartham. The Reverend Greatheed to whom this letter is addressed was a friend of Cowper's from 1785 until his death. Greatheed preached the funeral sermon for the poet in 1800.

My dear Sir,

Having first thanked you for your affectionate and acceptable letter, I will proceed, as well as I can, to answer your equally affectionate request that I would send you early news of our arrival at Eartham. Here we are in the most elegant mansion that I have ever inhabited, and surrounded by the most delightful pleasure grounds that I have ever seen; but which, dissipated as my powers of thought are at present, I will not undertake to describe. It shall suffice me to say that they occupy three sides of a hill, which in Buckinghamshire might well pass for a mountain, and from the summit of which is beheld a most magnificent landscape bounded by the sea, and in one part of it by the Isle of Wight, which may also be seen plainly from the window of the library in which I am writing.

It pleased God to carry us both through the journey with far less difficulty and inconvenience than I expected. I began it indeed with a thousand fears, and when we arrived the first evening at Barnet, found myself oppressed in spirit to a degree that could hardly be exceeded. I saw Mrs Unwin weary, as she might well be, and heard such a variety of noises, both within the house and without, that I concluded she would get no rest.

But I was mercifully disappointed. She rested, though not well, yet sufficiently; and when we finished our next day's journey at Ripley, we were both in better condition, both of body and mind, than on the day preceding. At Ripley we found a quiet inn, that housed, as it happened, that night, no company but ourselves. There we slept well, and rose perfectly refreshed. And except some terrors that I felt at passing over the Sussex hills by moonlight, met with little to complain of till we arrived about ten o'clock at Eartham. Here we are as happy as it is in the power of terrestrial good to make us. It is almost a Paradise in which we dwell; and our reception has been the kindest that it was possible for friendship and hospitality to contrive. Our host mentions you with great respect, and bids me tell you that he esteems you highly. Mrs Unwin, who is, I think, in some points, already the better for her excursion, unites with mine her best compliments both to yourself and Mrs Greatheed. I have much to see and enjoy before I can be perfectly apprised of all the delights of Eartham, and will therefore now subscribe myself, yours, my dear Sir, with great sincerity,

W.C.

CIX *To Samuel Rose*   9 November 1792

My dear Friend,

I wish that I were as industrious, and as much occupied as you, though in a different way; but it is not so with me. Mrs Unwin's great debility, (who is not yet able to move without assistance,) is of itself a hinderance such as would effectually disable me. Till she can work and read, and fill up her time as usual, (all which is at present entirely out of her power,) I may now and then find time to write a letter, but I shall write nothing more. I cannot sit with my pen in my hand, and my books before me, while she is in effect in solitude, silent, and looking at the fire. To this hinderance that other has been added, of which you are already aware, – a want of spirits, such as I have never known, when I was not absolutely laid by, since I commenced

145

an author. How long I shall be continued in these uncomfortable circumstances is known only to Him who, as he will, disposes of us all. I may be yet able perhaps to prepare the first book of the *Paradise Lost* for the press, before it will be wanted; and Johnson himself seems to think there will be no haste for the second. But poetry is my favourite employment, and all my poetical operations are in the mean time suspended; for while a work to which I have bound myself remains unaccomplished I can do nothing else.

Johnson's plan of prefixing my phiz to the new edition of my *Poems* is by no means a pleasant one to me, and so I told him in a letter I sent him from Eartham, in which I assured him that my objections to it would not be easily surmounted. But if you judge that it may really have an effect in advancing the sale, I would not be so squeamish as to suffer the spirit of prudery to prevail in me to his disadvantage. Somebody told an author, I forget whom, that there was more vanity in refusing his picture, than in granting it; on which he instantly complied. I do not perfectly feel all the force of the argument, but it shall content me that he did.

[...]

Adieu! We expect you at Christmas, and shall therefore rejoice when Christmas comes. Let nothing interfere. – Ever yours,

W.C.

CX *To Lady Hesketh*   1 December 1792

I am truly glad, my dearest coz, that the waters of Cheltenham have done thee good, and wish ardently that those of Bath may establish thy health, and prove the means of prolonging it many years, even till thou shalt become what thou wast called at a very early age, an old wench indeed. I have been a *pauvre miserable* ever since I came from Eartham, and was little better while there, so that whatever motive may incline me to travel again hereafter, it will not be the hope that my spirits will be much the better for it. Neither was Mrs Unwin's health so much improved by that frisk of ours into Sussex, as I had hoped and expected. She is, however, tolerably well, but very far indeed from having recovered the effects of her last disorder.

My birthday (the sixty-first that I have numbered) has proved for once a propitious day to me, for on that day my spirits began to mend, my nights became less hideous, and my days have been such of course.

[...]

I was never so idle in my life, and never had so much to do. God knows when this will end, but I think of bestirring myself soon, and of putting on my Miltonic trammels once again. That once done, I shall not, I hope, put them off till the work is finished. I have written nothing lately but a sonnet to Romney, and a mortuary copy of verses for the town of Northampton, having been applied to by the new clerk for that purpose.

Johnson designs handsomely; you must pardon Johnson, and receive him into your best graces. He purposes to publish, together with my Homer, a new edition of my two volumes of *Poems*, and to make me a present of the entire profits. They are to be handsome quartos, with an engraving of Abbott's picture of me prefixed. I have left myself neither time nor room for politics.

The French are a vain and childish people, and conduct themselves on this grand occasion with a levity and extravagance nearly akin to madness; but it would have been better for Austria and Prussia to let them alone. All nations have a right to choose their own mode of government, and the sovereignty of the people is a doctrine that evinces itself; for whenever the people choose to be masters they always are so, and none can hinder them. God grant that we may have no revolution here, but unless we have a reform, we certainly shall. Depend upon it, my dear, the hour is come when power founded in patronage and corrupt majorities must govern this land no longer. Concessions too must be made to dissenters of every denomination. They have a right to them, a right to all the privileges of Englishmen, and sooner or later, by fair means or by force, they will have them.

Adieu, my dearest coz, I have only time to add Mrs U's most affectionate remembrances, and to conclude myself ever thine,

Wm. Cowper

CXI *To William Hayley*   24 February 1793

Cowper signs this letter 'Lippus': 'a man with sore eyes'. As he states in the *Memoir*, he had had 'very weak eyes' from a young age, which caused such concern that he was sent to stay for some time with an eminent oculist when he was eight years old. In his later correspondence, and particularly as his final depression deepened, his concern with his failing and painful vision increased.

Your letter (so full of kindness, and so exactly in unison with my own feelings for you) should have had, as it deserved to have, an earlier answer, had I not been perpetually tormented with inflamed eyes, which are a sad hinderance to me in every thing. But to make amends, if I do not send you an early answer, I send you at least a speedy one, being obliged to write as fast as my pen can trot, that I may shorten the time of poring upon paper as much as possible. Homer too has been another hinderance, for always when I can see, which is only about two hours every morning, and not at all by candlelight, I devote myself to him, being in haste to send him a second time to the press, that nothing may stand in the way of Milton. [...]

Oh! you rogue! what would you give to have such a dream about Milton, as I had about a week since? I dreamed that being in a house in the city, and with much company, looking towards the lower end of the room from the upper end of it, I descried a figure which I immediately knew to be Milton's. He was very gravely, but very neatly attired in the fashion of his day, and had a countenance which filled me with those feelings that an affectionate child has for a beloved father, such, for instance, as Tom has for you. My first thought was wonder, where he could have been concealed so many years; my second, a transport of

148

joy to find him still alive; my third, another transport to find myself in his company; and my fourth, a resolution to accost him. I did so, and he received me with a complacence, in which I saw equal sweetness and dignity. I spoke of his *Paradise Lost*, as every man must, who is worthy to speak of it at all, and told him a long story of the manner in which it affected me, when I first discovered it, being at that time a schoolboy. He answered me by a smile and a gentle inclination of his head. He then grasped my hand affectionately, and with a smile that charmed me, said, 'Well, you for your part will do well also;' at last recollecting his great age, (for I understood him to be two hundred years old,) I feared that I might fatigue him by much talking, I took my leave, and he took his, with an air of the most perfect good breeding. His person, his features, his manner, were all so perfectly characteristic, that I am persuaded an apparition of him could not represent him more completely. This may be said to have been one of the dreams of Pindus, may it not?

[...]

With Mary's kind love, I must now conclude myself, my dear brother, ever yours,

Lippus

CXII *To Charlotte Smith*   25 July 1793

Charlotte Smith (1749–1806) was an extremely popular and talented writer who, although long neglected by critics, is now frequently credited (along with Cowper) as being one of the first Romantics. Already an admirer of *The Task*, she met Cowper during his visit to Eartham and dedicated her poem, *The Emigrants* (1793), to him. In this dedication she claims Cowper to be 'one of the few who, at the present period, rescue [England] from the imputation of having degenerated in poetical talents'.

My Dear Madam,
Many reasons concurred to make me impatient for the arrival

of your most acceptable present, and among them was the fear lest you should, perhaps, suspect me of tardiness in acknowledging so great a favour, – a fear that, as often as it prevailed, distressed me exceedingly. At length I have received it, and my little bookseller assures me that he sent it the very day he got it; by some mistake, however, the wagon brought it instead of the coach, which occasioned a delay that I could ill afford.

It came this morning about an hour ago; consequently I have not had time to peruse the poem, though you may be sure I have found enough for the perusal of the Dedication. I have in fact given it three readings, and in each have found increasing pleasure.

I am a whimsical creature; when I write for the public, I write, of course, with a desire to please, in other words, to acquire fame, and I labour accordingly; but when I find that I have succeeded, feel myself alarmed, and ready to shrink from the acquisition.

This I have felt more than once, and when I saw my name at the head of your Dedication, I felt it again; but the consummate delicacy of your praise soon convinced me that I might spare my blushes, and that the demand was less upon my modesty than my gratitude. Of that be assured, dear Madam, and of the truest esteem and respect of your most obliged and affectionate humble servant,

W.C.

[...]

CXIII *To John Johnson*   6 September 1793

My Dearest Johnny,

To do a kind thing, and in a kind manner, is a double kindness, and no man is more addicted to both than you, or more skilful in contriving them. Your plan to surprise me agreeably succeeded to admiration. It was only the day before yesterday that, while we walked after dinner in the orchard, Mrs Unwin between Sam and me, hearing the hall-clock, I observed a great difference between that and ours, and began immediately to lament, as I had often done, that there was not a sun-dial in all Weston to ascertain the true time for us. My complaint was long, and lasted till having turned into the grass walk, we reached the new building at the end of it; where we sat awhile and reposed ourselves. In a few minutes we returned by the way we came, when what think you was my astonishment to see what I had not seen before, though I had passed close by it, a smart sun-dial mounted on a smart stone pedestal! I assure you it seemed the effect of conjuration. I stopped short, and exclaimed, – 'Why, here is a sun-dial, and upon our ground! How is this? Tell me, Sam, how came it here? Do you know any thing about it?' At first I really thought (that is to say, as soon as I could think at all) that this factotum of mine, Sam Roberts, having often heard me deplore the want of one, had given orders for the supply of that want himself, without my knowledge, and was half pleased and half offended. But he soon exculpated himself by imputing the fact to you. It was brought up to Weston (it seems) about noon: but Andrews stopped the cart at the blacksmith's, whence he sent to inquire if I was gone for my walk. As it happened, I walked not till two o'clock. So there it stood waiting till I should go forth, and was introduced before my return. Fortunately too I went out at the church end of the village, and consequently saw nothing of it. How I could possibly pass it without seeing it, when it stood in the walk, I know not, but it is certain that I did. And where I shall fix it now, I know as little. It cannot stand between the two gates, the place of your choice, as I understand from Samuel, because the hay-cart must pass that way in the season. But we are now busy in winding the walk all round the orchard, and in doing so shall doubtless stumble at last upon some open spot that will suit it.

There it shall stand, while I live, a constant monument of your kindness.

I have this moment finished the twelfth book of the *Odyssey*; and I read the *Iliad* to Mrs Unwin every evening.

The effect of this reading is that I still spy blemishes, something at least that I can mend, so that after all, the transcript of alterations, which you and George have made, will not be a perfect one. It would be foolish to forego an opportunity of improvement for such a reason; neither will I. It is ten o'clock, and I must breakfast. Adieu, therefore, my dear Johnny! Remember your appointment to see us in October. – Ever yours,

W.C.

CXIV *To Lady Hesketh*   27 August 1795

At about the time Cowper returned to Weston from his visit to Hayley in Eartham, his mental and physical health began to deteriorate. By July 1795, he was so disturbed by fantasies about being carried away by evil spirits that Lady Hesketh and John Johnson decided it was necessary to move him and Mrs Unwin to Mundesley in Norfolk in order for them to be near (and under the supervision of) Johnson and the poet's maternal aunts. Despite the change in circumstances, Cowper's health continued to deteriorate and, although he lived for almost five more years, he never regained his former spirits.

Hopeless as ever, and chiefly to gratify myself by once more setting pen to paper, I address a very few lines to one whom it would be a comfort to me to gratify as much by sending them. The most forlorn of beings I tread a shore under the burthen of infinite despair, that I once trod all cheerfulness and joy. I view every vessel that approaches the coast with an eye of jealousy and fear, lest it arrive with a commission to seize me. But my insensibility, which you say is a mystery to you, because it seems incompatible with such fear, has the effect of courage, and enables me to go forth, as if on purpose to place myself in the way of danger. The cliff is here of a height that it is terrible to look down from; and yesterday evening, by moonlight, I passed sometimes within a foot of the edge of it, from which to have fallen would probably have been to be dashed in pieces. But though to have been dashed in pieces would perhaps have been best for me, I shrunk from the precipice, and am waiting

152

to be dashed in pieces by other means. At two miles distance on the coast is a solitary pillar of rock, that the crumbling cliff has left at the high water- mark. I have visited it twice, and have found it an emblem of myself. Torn from my natural connexions, I stand alone and expect the storm that shall displace me.

I have no expectation that I shall ever see you more, though Samuel assures me that I shall visit Weston again, and that you will meet me there. My terrors, when I left it, would not permit me to say – Farewell for ever – which now I do; wishing, but vainly wishing to see you yet once more, and equally wishing that I could now as confidently, and as warmly as once I could, subscribe myself affectionately yours; but every feeling that would warrant the doing it, has, as you too well know, long since forsaken the bosom of

W.C.

Mr Johnson is gone to North Walsham, and knows not that I write.

Mrs Unwin sends her affectionate respects and compliments.

CXV *To John Buchanan*   5 September 1795

The Reverend John Buchanan was the curate of Weston Underwood. The letter opens with a slightly amended citation from Milton's *Lycidas* (lines 152–3).

– to interpose a little ease,
Let my frail thoughts dally with false surmise!

I will forget for a moment, that to whomsoever I may address myself, a letter from me can no otherwise be welcome, than as a curiosity. To you, Sir, I address this; urged to it by extreme penury of employment, and the desire I feel to learn something of what is doing, and has been done at Weston (my beloved Weston!) since I left it.

The coldness of these blasts, even in the hottest days, has

been such, that added to the irritation of the salt spray, with which they are always charged, they have occasioned me an inflammation in the eyelids, which threatened a few days since to confine me entirely; but absenting myself as much as possible from the beach, and guarding my face with an umbrella, that inconvenience is in some degree abated. My chamber commands a very near view of the ocean, and the ships at high water approach the coast so closely, that a man furnished with better eyes than mine might, I doubt not, discern the sailors from the window. No situation, at least when the weather is clear and bright, can be pleasanter; which you will easily credit, when I add that it imparts something a little resembling pleasure even to me. – Gratify me with news from Weston! If Mr Gregson, and your neighbours the Courtenays are there, mention me to them in such terms as you see good. Tell me if my poor birds are living? I never see the herbs I used to give them without a recollection of them, and sometimes am ready to gather them, forgetting that I am not at home. Pardon this intrusion!

Mrs Unwin continues much as usual.

CXVI *To Lady Hesketh*   26 September 1795

Mr Johnson is gone forth again, and again, for the last time I suppose that I shall ever do it, I address a line to you. I knew not of his intentions to leave me till the day before he did so. Like every thing else that constitutes my wretched lot, this departure of his was sudden, and shocked me accordingly. He enjoined me before he went, if I wrote at all in his absence, to write to Mr Newton. But I cannot, and so I told him. Whither he is gone I know not; at least I know not by information from himself. Samuel tells me that he thinks his destination is to Weston. But why to Weston is unimaginable to me. I shall never see Weston more. I have been tossed like a ball into a far country, from which there is no rebound for me. There indeed I lived a life of infinite despair, and such is my life in Norfolk.

Such indeed it would be in any given spot upon the face of the globe; but to have passed the little time that remained to me there, was the desire of my heart. My heart's desire however has been always frustrated in every thing that it ever settled on, and by means that have made my disappointments inevitable. When I left Weston I despaired of reaching Norfolk, and now that I have reached Norfolk, I am equally hopeless of ever reaching Weston more. What a lot is mine! Why was existence given to a creature that might possibly, and would probably become wretched in the degree that I have been so? and whom misery, such as mine, was almost sure to overwhelm in a moment. But the question is vain. I existed by a decree from which there was no appeal, and on terms the most tremendous, because unknown to, and even unsuspected by me; difficult to be complied with had they been foreknown, and unforeknown, impracticable. Of this truth I have no witness but my own experience; a witness, whose testimony will not be admitted. But farewell to a subject with which I can only weary you, and blot the paper to no purpose.

You assure me that I shall see you again; tell me where and when, I shall see you, and I will believe you if it be possible.

Samuel desires me to present his duty to you. His wife is gone to Weston, and he wishes me to say that if Mrs Herbert has any concerns there that Nanny can settle for her, and will give her the necessary directions, she may depend upon their being exactly attended to. With Mrs Unwin's respects, I remain the forlorn and miserable being I was when I wrote last.

W.C.

On 17 December 1797, Mary Unwin died. Cowper's melancholy continued to worsen until his own death on 25 April 1800.

Dear Cousin,

You describe delightful scenes, but you describe them to one who, if he even saw them, could receive no delight from them, – who has a faint recollection, and so faint as to be like an almost forgotten dream, that once he was susceptible of pleasure from such causes. The country that you have had in prospect has been always famed for its beauties; but the wretch who can derive no gratification from a view of nature, even under the disadvantage of her most ordinary dress, will have no eyes to admire her in any. In one day, in one moment I should rather have said, she became an *universal blank* to me, and, though from a different cause, yet with an effect as difficult to remove, as blindness itself. In this country, if there are not mountains, there are hills; if not broad and deep rivers, yet such as are sufficient to embellish a prospect; and an object still more magnificent than any river, the ocean itself, is almost immediately under the window. Why is scenery like this, I had almost said, why is the very scene, which many years since I could not contemplate without rapture, now become, at the best, an insipid wilderness to me? It neighbours nearly, and as nearly resembles the scenery of Catfield; but with what different perceptions does it present me! The reason is obvious. My state of mind is a medium through which the beauties of Paradise itself could not be communicated with any effect but a painful one.

There is a wide interval between us, which it would be far easier for you than for me to pass. Yet I should in vain invite you. We shall meet no more. I know not what Mr Johnson said of me in the long letter he addressed to you yesterday, but nothing, I am sure, that could make such an event seem probable. – I remain as usual, dear cousin, yours,

Wm. Cowper

Index of Correspondents
to Whom the Letters are Addressed

Fyfield Books

BORDER BALLADS
A Selection
edited by James Reed

FIVE FATHERS
Five Australian Poets of the
Pre-Academic Era
edited by Les Murray

POETRY BY ENGLISH WOMEN
Elizabethan to Victorian
edited by R. E. Pritchard

THE POORHOUSE FUGITIVES
Self-Taught Poets and Poetry
in Victorian Britain
edited by Brian Maidment

LANCELOT ANDREWES
(1555–1626)
Selected Writings
edited by P.E. Hewison

MATTHEW ARNOLD
(1822–1888)
Selected Poems
edited by Keith Silver

JANE AUSTEN (1775–1817)
Collected Poems and Verse of
the Austen Family
edited by David Selwyn

Jane Austen: a Celebration
*edited by Maggie Lane and
David Selwyn*

WILLIAM BARNES
(1801–1886)
Selected Poems
edited by Robert Nye

THOMAS L. BEDDOES
(1803–1849)
Selected Poetry
*edited by Judith Higgens
and Michael Bradshaw*

APHRA BEHN (1640–1689)
Selected Poems
edited by Malcolm Hicks

EDMUND BLUNDEN
(1896–1974)
Selected Poems
edited by Robyn Marsack

THE BRONTË SISTERS
Selected Poems of Charlotte,
Emily and Anne Brontë
edited by Stevie Davies

SIR THOMAS BROWNE
(1605–1682)
Selected Writings
edited by Claire Preston

ELIZABETH BARRETT
BROWNING
(1806–1861)
Selected Poems
edited by Malcolm Hicks

THOMAS CAMPION
(1567–1620)
Ayres and Observations
edited by Joan Hart

LEWIS CARROLL (1832–1898)
Selected Poems
edited by Keith Silver

THOMAS CHATTERTON
(1752–1770)
Selected Poems
edited by Grevel Lindop

JOHN CLARE (1793–1864)
Northborough Sonnets
*Edited by Eric Robinson, David
Powell and P.M.S. Dawson*

The Midsummer Cushion
*edited by R.K.R. Thornton
and Anne Tibble*

John Clare by Himself
*edited by Eric Robinson
and David Powell*

ARTHUR HUGH CLOUGH
(1819–1861)
Selected Poems
edited by Shirley Chew

SAMUEL TAYLOR COLERIDGE
(1772–1834)
Selected Poetry
*edited by William Empson
and David Pirie*

CHARLES COTTON
(1630–1687)
Selected Poems
edited by Ken Robinson

ABRAHAM COWLEY
(1618–1667)
Selected Poems
*edited by David Hopkins
and Tom Mason*

WILLIAM COWPER
(1731–1800)
Selected Poems
edited by Nicholas Rhodes

Selected Letters
edited by Simon Malpas

GEORGE CRABBE (1754–1832)
Selected Poems
edited by Jem Poster

WILLIAM DUNBAR
(?1460–1520?)
Selected Poems
edited by H. Harvey Wood

ANNE FINCH, COUNTESS OF
WINCHILSEA (1661–1720)
Selected Poems
edited by Denys Thompson

JOHN GAY (1685–1732)
Selected Poems
edited by Marcus Walsh

OLIVER GOLDSMITH
(?1730–1774)
Selected Poems
edited by John Lucas

JOHN GOWER (1330–1408)
Selected Poetry
edited by Carole Weinberg

THOMAS GRAY (1716–1771)
Selected Poems
edited by John Heath-Stubbs

FULKE GREVILLE (1554–1628)
Selected Poems
edited by Neil Powell

IVOR GURNEY (1890–1937)
Best Poems *and*
The Book of Five Makings
edited by R.K.R. Thornton

Severn and Somme *and*
War's Embers
edited by R.K.R. Thornton

80 Poems or So
edited by R.K.R. Thornton
and George Walter

Rewards of Wonder
edited by George Walter

ROBERT HENRYSON
(?1425–1508?)
Selected Poems
edited by W.R.J. Barron

ROBERT HERRICK (1591–1674)
Selected Poems
edited by David Jesson-Dibley

THOMAS HOOD (1799–1845)
Selected Poems
edited by Joy Flint

RICHARD HOOKER
(1553/4–1600)
Ecclesiastical Polity:
selections
edited by Arthur Pollard

LEIGH HUNT (1784–1859)
Selected Writings
edited by David Jesson-Dibley

BEN JONSON (1572–1637)
Epigrams & The Forest
edited by Richard Dutton

CHARLES LAMB (1775–1834)
Charles Lamb and Elia
edited by J.E. Morpurgo

HUGH LATIMER (1490–1555)
Sermons
edited by Arthur Pollard

WILLIAM LAW (1686–1761)
Selected Writings
edited by Janet Louth

RICHARD LOVELACE
(1618–1658)
Selected Poems
edited Gerald Hammond

JOHN LYLY (1554?–1606)
Selected Prose and Dramatic
Work
edited by Leah Scragg

ANDREW MARVELL
(1621–1678)
Selected Poems
edited by Bill Hutchings

JOHN MASEFIELD (1878–1967)
Selected Poems
edited by Donald Stanford

CHARLOTTE MEW
(1869–1928)
Collected Poems and
Selected Prose
edited by Val Warner

WILLIAM MORRIS
(1834–1896)
Selected Poems
edited by Peter Faulkner

EDGAR ALLAN POE
(1809–1849)
Poems and Essays on Poetry
edited by C.H. Sisson

CHRISTINA ROSSETTI
(1830–1894)
Selected Poems
edited by C.H. Sisson

DANTE GABRIEL ROSSETTI
(1828–1892)
Selected Poems and
Translations
edited by Clive Wilmer

SIR WALTER SCOTT
(1771–1832)
Selected Poems
edited by James Reed

MARY SIDNEY, COUNTESS OF
PEMBROKE (1561–1621) and
SIR PHILIP SIDNEY (1554–1586)
The Sidney Psalms
edited by R.E. Pritchard

SIR PHILIP SIDNEY
(1554–1586)
Selected Writings
edited by Richard Dutton

JOHN SKELTON (1460–1529)
Selected Poems
edited by Gerald Hammond

HENRY HOWARD, EARL OF
SURREY
(1517–1547)
Selected Poems
edited by Dennis Keene

JONATHAN SWIFT
(1667–1745)
Selected Poems
edited by C.H. Sisson

ALGERNON CHARLES
SWINBURNE
(1837–1909)
Selected Poems
edited by L.M. Findlay

ARTHUR SYMONS
(1865–1945)
Selected Writings
edited by R.V. Holdsworth

JEREMY TAYLOR (1613–1667)
Selected Writings
edited by C.H. Sisson

THOMAS TRAHERNE
(?1637–1674)
Select Meditations
edited by Julia J. Smith

HENRY VAUGHAN
(1622–1695)
Selected Poems
edited by Robert B. Shaw

IZAAK WALTON (1593–1683)
Selected Writings
edited by Jessica Martin

ISAAC WATTS (1674–1748)
Selected Poems
edited by Gordon Jackson

JAMES MCNEIL WHISTLER
(1834–1903)
Whistler on Art
edited by Nigel Thorp

OSCAR WILDE (1854–1900)
Selected Poems
edited by Malcolm Hicks

SIR THOMAS WYATT
(1503–1542)
Selected Poems
edited by Hardiman Scott

'Carcanet are doing an excellent job in this series: the editions are labours of love, not just commercial enterprises. I hope they are familiar to all readers and teachers of literature.' – *Times Literary Supplement*